HOW TO MAKE A LIVING WRITING ARTICLES FOR NEWSPAPERS, MAGAZINES, AND ONLINE SOURCES

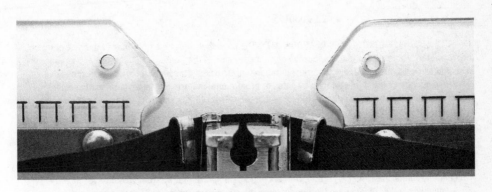

Everything You Need to know to Become a Successful Freelance Writer in 30 Days

Wendy Vincent

HOW TO MAKE A LIVING WRITING ARTICLES FOR NEWSPAPERS, MAGAZINES, AND ONLINE SOURCES: EVERYTHING YOU NEED TO KNOW TO BECOME A SUCCESSFUL FREELANCE WRITER IN 30 DAYS

Copyright © 2014 Atlantic Publishing Group, Inc.
1405 SW 6th Avenue • Ocala, Florida 34471 • Phone 800-814-1132 • Fax 352-622-1875
Website: www.atlantic-pub.com • Email: sales@atlantic-pub.com
SAN Number: 268-1250

Library of Congress Cataloging-in-Publication Data

Vincent, Wendy M., 1975-
How to make a living writing articles for newspapers, magazines, and online sources : everything you need to know to become a successful freelance writer in 30 days / by Wendy Vincent.
p. cm.
Includes bibliographical references and index.
ISBN 978-1-60138-567-3 (alk. paper) -- ISBN 1-60138-567-6 (alk. paper)
1. Authorship--Vocational guidance. 2. Freelance journalism--Vocational guidance. 3. Feature writing--Vocational guidance. I. Title.
PN151.V56 2012
808.02023--dc23
                    2012030165

Printed in the United States

INTERIOR LAYOUT: Antoinette D'Amore • addesign@videotron.ca
FRONT & BACK COVER DESIGNS: Jackie Miller • millerjackiej@gmail.com

Printed on Recycled Paper

A few years back we lost our beloved pet dog Bear, who was not only our best and dearest friend but also the "Vice President of Sunshine" here at Atlantic Publishing. He did not receive a salary but worked tirelessly 24 hours a day to please his parents.

Bear was a rescue dog who turned around and showered myself, my wife, Sherri, his grandparents Jean, Bob, and Nancy, and every person and animal he met (well, maybe not rabbits) with friendship and love. He made a lot of people smile every day.

We wanted you to know a portion of the profits of this book will be donated in Bear's memory to local animal shelters, parks, conservation organizations, and other individuals and nonprofit organizations in need of assistance.

– Douglas & Sherri Brown

PS: We have since adopted two more rescue dogs: first Scout, and the following year, Ginger. They were both mixed golden retrievers who needed a home.

Want to help animals and the world? Here are a dozen easy suggestions you and your family can implement today:

- *Adopt and rescue a pet from a local shelter.*
- *Support local and no-kill animal shelters.*
- *Plant a tree to honor someone you love.*
- *Be a developer — put up some birdhouses.*
- *Buy live, potted Christmas trees and replant them.*
- *Make sure you spend time with your animals each day.*
- *Save natural resources by recycling and buying recycled products.*
- *Drink tap water, or filter your own water at home.*
- *Whenever possible, limit your use of or do not use pesticides.*
- *If you eat seafood, make sustainable choices.*
- *Support your local farmers market.*
- *Get outside. Visit a park, volunteer, walk your dog, or ride your bike.*

Five years ago, Atlantic Publishing signed the Green Press Initiative. These guidelines promote environmentally friendly practices, such as using recycled stock and vegetable-based inks, avoiding waste, choosing energy-efficient resources, and promoting a no-pulping policy. We now use 100-percent recycled stock on all our books. The results: in one year, switching to post-consumer recycled stock saved 24 mature trees, 5,000 gallons of water, the equivalent of the total energy used for one home in a year, and the equivalent of the greenhouse gases from one car driven for a year.

DEDICATION

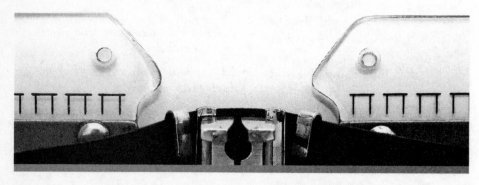

*This book is dedicated to my fellow writers
who continue to inspire me through their own dedication,
perseverance, and pure love of the written word.
I would also like to thank everyone who helped contribute
to this book and those who continue to strive towards
their own dreams of becoming writers.*

TABLE OF CONTENTS

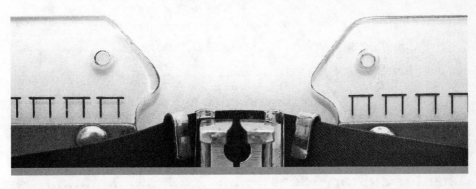

INTRODUCTION

"Most writers end up where they do by a series of accidents. The trick is to choose the right accidents."

— David Bouchier, *NY Times* columnist, award-winning essayist for NPR, and author of several books

I fell into writing almost by accident. I originally set out to be a news anchor. You know, one of those bobbleheads that looks perfectly coiffed while they read the news off the teleprompter from behind the desk. Perhaps, I even would conduct sit-down interviews with the likes of presidents, dignitaries, and the rich and famous from the comfort of their living room sofas. I even could have been a foreign correspondent who traveled the world and did exposés on starving children. While looking into the camera, a tear would roll down my cheek, and I would ask for you, the viewer sitting at home, to help save these destitute children.

What originally drew me to that profession was twofold: being able to travel as part of my work and uncovering people's true stories. As luck would have it, my life took a few different turns and twists, and I ended up as a writer. Better yet? I get to do just that. I have the freedom to travel around for my "job," and I get to uncover great stories. I don't even have to change out of my pajamas to go to work in the morning, the coffee pot has become my favorite home appliance, and I get paid to do something I love. Not many people can say that.

People often ask me how I became a writer and what advice I would offer to others to help them get started. The road for me was not as direct as setting out to become a writer. There are no clear-cut turns on the road to becoming a successful freelance writer. In my case, I pursued a bachelor's degree in communications with a minor in international languages and cultures. My goal back then was still to become a newsperson. What going to college did provide me with were the basic skills of writing, as I had to write numerous college papers as a communications major. One of the first steps to being a successful writer is to know how to write. Grammar, spelling, and being familiar with some basic writing styles will go a long way in getting hired. In Chapter 2, I will help you get started with the basics so you can begin your process. Writers write, and good writers know how to write.

After college, I worked in video for a while: first, at a production company, then at an international videoconferencing company. Both jobs allotted me the opportunity to learn how to be a successful project manager, a skill that comes in handy when you are juggling several clients as a writer. In reading this book, you will become familiar with the operations end of becoming a freelance writer from how to organize your workspace to contracts and invoicing. In essence, you will learn how to become a successful project manager — another key step in making a living as a writer.

I later worked in the corporate world of public relations and marketing where I learned the importance of how to market oneself. In the world of corporate communications, I was able to flex my writing skills while effectively selling a product. This book will provide you with some ideas and tools to be able to promote your writing skills effectively. From developing a portfolio to creating a Web page, you will learn how to "sell" yourself as a writer to continue getting writing jobs.

After I discovered the corporate world of 9 to 5 was not for me, I later returned to school and got my master's degree in liberal studies. My non-definitive master's degree is what actually led me to my first freelance job as a writer. Because the degree was general, I could choose any thesis topic to my liking, as long as I got it approved through the department head. I did my final master's thesis on the trobairitz, female troubadours from 12th and 13th century Occitania France. (As a side note, I have always loved medieval studies.) My work on this project led me to wonder if there was another outlet for all of the research I had just done. As a result, I hit the Internet and began searching for someone who might be interested in my work.

What I discovered was *Renaissance Magazine*. I read their instructions on sending in a query and followed it to the letter. Soon after, I got a response: They were willing to buy an article on my trobairitz. My writing career blossomed from there. For the past decade, I have been writing magazine articles, book reviews, online stories, résumés, travel articles, news stories, fliers, brochures, corporate materials, and a variety of other projects. I also currently am working on finishing my fourth book with three more in the works. In addition, I am an editor for an online news source, which has put me at the other end of the writing business — I am responsible for hiring freelancers and helping them perfect their craft. I have learned a lot about how to find writing jobs, getting jobs, and maintaining clients. And, I know first-hand what editors look for when contracting with a freelancer.

Keeping up with the business of writing is also about understanding the current trends. The world of writing has changed in the last decade. At one time, for example, sending in SASEs (self-addressed stamped envelopes) along with your query letters was mandatory. Nowadays, most clients prefer to communicate electronically and no longer ask for a SASE. A handful of others, however, still require you to communicate through snail mail. Understanding how to find clients specific guidelines and follow them to the letter is a key part to being a successful freelance writer.

Jobs no longer are found in black and white in the classifieds section of a print newspaper, but in the colorful world of cyberspace. The modern writer is savvy enough to be up to date on email communication and understands the importance of having a website and a blog. Even the newsroom has gone mobile. Journalists no longer are sitting in an office lineup of other journalists. Instead, they are working out of their houses, cars, or in coffee shops, where they wirelessly upload news stories to online news sites and use their smart phones to tweet from the sidelines of a soccer game.

Throughout this book, I will take you on a journey into the world of freelance writing. I hope to encourage you to pursue your dreams of being a writer while learning how to draw on your own personal past experiences to get there. There is no formal training to become a writer. Writers come from a variety of backgrounds. What we all share is a passion for what we do and a basic knowledge of the business. Learning some basic skills, writing everyday, getting organized, negotiating the current trends of the business, and learning how to market yourself will be the keys to your writing success.

This book will take you through the process of getting started on your successful freelance writing career. I hope it will become an invaluable resource on your writer's desk, and to that end, I have included a goal-setting worksheet, listing of writer resources and organizations, and a glossary of writing terms at the end of the book as a quick reference guide.

Enjoy the journey, and happy writing!

Chapter 1

A DAY IN THE LIFE

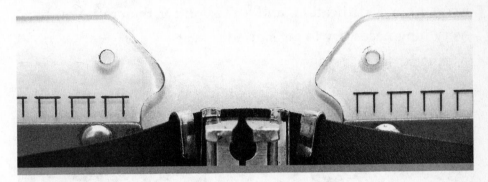

"The only thing I was fit for was to be a writer, and this notion rested solely on my suspicion that I would never be fit for real work, and that writing didn't require any."

— Russell Baker, American Pulitzer Prize-winning writer

Writing for a living is an amazing career. As a writer, you get to make your own hours, be your own boss, and flex your creative muscles, and you can work from anywhere. You can work around your family and still hold down a traditional day job while getting started. It lets you inspire, motive, educate, and maybe even change the world with a few carefully crafted sentences. Seeing your name in print or in a byline online can be as thrilling as bungee jumping from a bridge. Writing, however, is a much safer endeavor than free falling from a bridge. There are no special degrees, no particular career path choices, and no certifications required to become a freelance writer. If you have a computer, or access to one, dedication, and a passion for the craft, you have everything necessary to get started.

A freelance writer can be:

- An overworked corporate manager who is climbing the walls of his or her cubicle and just wants to work from home doing something more personally fulfilling than clocking hours in an office setting

- A stay-at-home mom who left the corporate world to stay home with her children but would like to get back to work in a creative way that would earn some extra income while having the flexibility to work around her family

- An accidental freelancer who was laid-off from a job due to a downturn in the economy and wants the security of being his or her own boss

- A person who wants to make some extra income while continuing to work at their current job

- Someone who is housebound due to an illness and is looking for a way to earn an income

The freelance model brings a new definition to the idea of "work." People are beginning to question the meaning of *work* in our lives. There seems to be a far-reaching awakening to the downsides of the traditional model of the 9-to-5 or shift-work-scheduled day. Is the corporate world worth the daily struggle and hours spent away from our families? Could we survive on less income but enjoy a better quality of life? Is it worth it to pay for day care for children when we could work fewer hours and spend more time with the kids? Many professionals have grown tired of long commutes, 50-plus-hour workweeks, and carefully rationed vacation and sick time. Employees are weary of going to work each day wondering if they will be the next people downsized as major corporations continue to cut costs.

From a business standpoint, companies are able to save money by hiring freelancers. They can pay for jobs on a per contract basis and do not have to pay a full salary or the added costs of benefits. Hiring freelancers also gives companies the flexibility to hire people with specific talents on an as-needed basis. Overall, the world of freelancing quickly is becoming the place where business is conducted.

With all the positives of being a freelance writer, you also have some important details to consider. Freelance writing is not for the faint of heart. Rejections are a part of the process, and every writer will be rejected multiple times throughout his or her career. Writing is not as simple as being creative. Sometimes the words will not flow when you want them to. Also, freelance writing is a business. As such, it requires work. Being your own project manager and dealing with mundane tasks such as invoicing, filing, and communicating with clients will also be a big part of the job. Keeping up on current trends and spending hours doing research are part of the job description. You also will need the discipline to schedule your work and not be tempted by things that might distract you from writing, such as the television or watching funny videos on YouTube®. On the other hand, you will be able to throw in a load of laundry before heading to your desk to write and schedule your workday around the kids' soccer games.

Do you think you are ready?

What is a Freelance Writer?

The term freelancer is used to describe someone who is self-employed and contracts him or herself out on a job-by-job basis. The company does not employ this person formally nor offer him or her the benefits of an employee. Instead, a freelancer contracts for a specific job in exchange for a certain rate of pay. In the terms of a freelance writer, this person will contract with a particular client for a specific writing job at an agreed-upon rate of pay. Often, freelance writers develop lasting relationships with clients and will work on a variety of projects.

> The word freelancer is derived from the term "free-lance." The term was used to describe a medieval mercenary warrior. It is often attributed to Sir Walter Scott, who used the term in his novel, *Ivanhoe* in the year 1820.

The challenge from a writer's standpoint is how to create a viable freelance writing business that is flexible and well-balanced yet provides a means to make money to pay for the mortgage, the electric bills, groceries, and those family vacations. Being a freelance writer does require a commitment on your part and a willingness to put in the effort to make it a viable career path. Despite the images you might have of what it might mean to be a freelance writer, a freelance writer is NOT:

- Someone who puts in an hour and spends the rest of the day on the beach every day. (The job does allow the flexibility to do this on occasion, but doing it every day will not help pay the bills.)

- Someone who does one small project and rakes in enough money to take the rest of the year off. Freelance writing requires work. Often, while working on a project, you will be spending your free time looking for the next project.

Instead, a freelance writer is:

- Someone who sets aside time each day to actively pursue writing opportunities

- Someone who spends time communicating with clients, sending correspondences, filing paperwork, and running the business end

- Someone who has the ability to work from anywhere and make his or her own hours

- Someone who can work in his or her pajamas if they want to

- Someone who can work the jobs around the needs of the family or other responsibilities

- Someone who has a passion for the written word and enjoys a creative job

Do you think you have what it takes?

Start by answering the following questions:

1. Do you have the time to pursue writing as a career?

2. If not, are you willing to rearrange your life to find the time to pursue writing?

3. What skills do you bring to writing? (i.e. special knowledge on a subject, college degree, writing experience, dedication to learn, good knowledge of grammar, etc.)

4. Are you willing to work hard at making it as a writer?

Starting a freelance writing career does not have to mean quitting your 9-to-5 job and jumping in headfirst. Although, it has been done, most people prefer the security of easing their way in and building up a few bylines first to get going.

What qualities do freelance writers have?

Freelance writers do not come from a specific background. Some may have started out as English or communication majors in college, but most have no formal training in the writing arena. Many are people burned-out on their current careers and are looking for a major change to work on something more creative.

Learning how to use your specific skills and interests is the key to becoming a successful freelance writer. For example, a computer programmer might find herself writing niche writing for online technology sites and magazines. A CPA who spends his free time cooking and attending wine pairing classes might become a successful paid blogger in the foodie arena. Someone who is working at an office job but is involved in local politics might find success writing hot-button political columns for a local newspaper.

The lesson here is that no specific requirements are set in stone as to what background you need to become a freelance writer. The great thing about freelance writing as a career is it does not have a laundry list of prerequisites. What you do need to be a freelance writer however, is the following:

- **Writing ability:** Freelance writers get hired because they are good writers. One of the keys to being a good writer is to acknowledge that no matter where you are in writing, you can always be a better writer. The craft can be perfected over and over again.

- **Professionalism:** Freelance writers continue to get job after job because they are professionals. Learning how to send queries, handle correspondence, work with editors, meet deadlines, and negotiate contracts while behaving courteously and professionally are necessary in this business.

- **Good business sense:** Writing, albeit a creative process, is ultimately a business. A good freelancer knows how to develop and sell materials for publication. He or she also knows how to conduct research and keep up with current trends. Writers must be willing and able to file, keep expenses, and maintain job files and client correspondences.

- **Motivation and Desire:** Many people desire to be freelance writers, but those who are truly motivated are the ones who succeed. Working at becoming a freelancer requires making changes in your lifestyle to attain your goals. For example, it might mean finding the motivation to get up a few hours before the rest of your household to write. It might mean giving up watching television at the end of the day so you can squeeze in some extra hours of writing time. You will write when you do not feel like writing; you probably will write about topics you hate but need to stretch your abilities for that next client. You will have to convince your family to learn to respect your writing time, especially when you work at home. You will have to be motivated to keep plowing through even when your parents continue to ask you when you are going to "get a real job."

- **Discipline:** Because freelance writers are their own bosses, no one is there to tell you when or how to get your job done. You set the deadlines, and you must hit them to succeed.

Who needs freelance writers?

A freelance writer can write for a variety of publications and markets. Some examples might include:

- **Print newspapers:** Hundreds of newspapers across the country are open to freelance contributions. Newspapers always look for the local angle, so writing for newspapers will need to be locale-specific. Newspapers take a variety of articles but might not pay as much as magazines do. They also work on shorter timelines than magazines and other forms of writing.

- **Print magazines:** Magazines are believed to represent the highest-paying and most accessible freelance writer market. Thousands of print magazines in the United States alone accept work from freelance writers.

- **Online:** Web page copy, webzines, feature articles, how-to articles, blogs, and hotel reviews are just a few of the many online writing options out there. Writing on the Web can vary greatly in payment from pennies per click to hundreds for website copy.

- **Business:** Writing for large corporations often provides steadier work due to the large pool and variety of job opportunities available. Corporations, in an effort to save costs, now outsource many of their writing needs. Types of projects they typically look for freelancers to help with might include newsletters, press releases, website copy, case studies, ad copy, quality control manuals, form letters, and business proposals.

- **Books:** Few freelancers begin their writing career by writing books. Usually, books are the next step after you have some experience being published in magazines, newspapers, and online. This does not mean you have to write the next best seller to make money from writing books. Beginning writers do have the opportunity, however, to work directly with publishers on a contract basis. In other words, the publisher dictates the title and information they would like included in the book, and the writers agrees to a flat fee for the work. These types of book-writing deals usually do not include royalties.

In essence, a freelance writer can come from a variety of backgrounds and still be successful. A day in the life of a freelance writer, however, is as varied as the people themselves.

A Day in the Life of a Freelance Writer

The benefit to being a freelance writer is that no two days are ever alike. Some days can be spent writing for hours; others, it seems as if nary a word is typed or written down. Some days are filled with responding to email, sending query letters, and filing. Others are spent tackling household chores in between firing off a sentence or two on a current project. Occasionally, if one is lucky, a day might be spent amongst the stacks at the local library researching a new topic. Another freelance writer might spend a typical 9-to-5 workday at their full-time job and sit down to do some writing at the end of the day, long after the sun has set. A typical day in the life of a freelance writer will depend greatly upon that particular person's approach to the job. The two biggest factors that affect how a freelance writer spends his or her time is whether he or she is working as a freelancer on a full-time or part-time basis and how that person organizes time to get the tasks done. Another piece to the puzzle is creating a healthy work-life balance with your writing career.

Full-time freelance writer path

A full-time freelance writer is someone who is a freelance writer all of the time and does not rely on another full-time job for income. This person's workday is filled with tasks directly related to his or her freelance writing career and can include writing, sending correspondences, bill paying, sending query letters, and other job-related tasks. Following are a couple of examples of a typical day in the life of a full-time freelance writer. Note that a "typical" day can vary greatly from day to day and is completely dependent upon the individual freelance writer. The following examples, however, will provide a general idea of what full-time freelance writers can expect their days to look like.

Scenario One: Full-time freelance writer and stay-at-home parent

5:30 a.m.	Walk on treadmill for 30 minutes.
6:00 a.m.	Take shower and get dressed.
6:30 a.m.	Make school lunches, get children ready for school, have breakfast with the family.
7:30 a.m.	Drop kids off at the bus stop and partner at the train station.
8:30 a.m.	Arrive back home, throw in a load of laundry, and get dinner in the Crock-Pot®.
9:30 a.m.	Make a cup of coffee and settle in at work desk to check and respond to emails, send a tweet, and update Facebook® status.
11:00 a.m.	Research topic for newspaper essay due today by 5 p.m.
12:00 a.m.	Remember to go change laundry and grab something for lunch.
12:30 p.m.	Settle back in at desk, check emails again, send another tweet, update Facebook, and start writing newspaper column.
2:00 p.m.	Put column aside for a bit and take a stretching break from sitting.

2:30 p.m.	Check email again, make phone call to a client wanting an update on a magazine piece.
3:00 p.m.	Proofread newspaper column and send it off to editor, along with invoice.
3:30 p.m.	Update list of current projects and adjust personal working calendar for the week.
4:00 p.m.	Meet children at the bus stop.
4:30 p.m.	Help kids with homework.
5:30 p.m.	Pick up partner at train station.
6:00 p.m.	Sit down to family dinner.
7:00 p.m.	Get outfits ready for school tomorrow and fold laundry. Spend time with the children playing games, cleaning their rooms, reading with them, and helping them get ready for bed with baths.
9:00 p.m.	After everyone is in bed, make a cup of tea, grab a cookie, and sit down with partner on couch to check email, respond to anything important, send a tweet, update Facebook, and search for writing jobs.
10:30 p.m.	Drift off to sleep.

Scenario Two: Full-time freelance writer just laid-off from full-time corporate job

6:00 a.m.	Head to the local gym and work out for an hour.
7:30 a.m.	Come home, take a shower, and grab breakfast.
8:30 a.m.	Settle in at work desk with a cup of coffee. Respond to email, research writing jobs on the Internet, write and send several queries for story ideas.
10:00 a.m.	Make phone calls to past coworkers to find out if anyone is in need of writing services.
11:00 a.m.	Sign up with an Internet company to purchase a website domain to host a website for a writing business. Research best ways to create a website.
12:30 p.m.	Meet a friend for lunch who has been a freelance writer for several years to pick his brain on the business of writing.

2:30 p.m.	Head to the local library to pick up some guidebooks on creating a successful writing business.
4:00 p.m.	Come home, check email, sign up for Twitter® and Facebook accounts, and make a list of ideas for website.
6:00 p.m.	Grab dinner.
7:00 p.m.	Watch television.
10:00 p.m.	Sit down to check email, write some story ideas down, and make a list of possible magazines and newspapers to sell the ideas to.
11:30 p.m.	Drift off to sleep after catching the evening news.

Part-time freelance writer journey

Typical part-time freelance writers have "day jobs." In other words, they work full time somewhere else and pursue their writing careers on the side. This person might be starting out as a writer or might have decided to work full time and pursue writing on the side because he or she enjoys the security of a full-time job elsewhere. Like full-time freelance writers, a typical day can vary greatly from freelancer to freelancer. Below are a couple of examples to provide you with a better understanding of what a part-time freelancer might do in a typical day.

Scenario A: Full-time information technology director, part-time freelance writer

6:00 a.m.	Get up, take shower, grab breakfast, and head to train station.
7:30 a.m.	Catch train to work and work on a technology article due by the end of the week for a computer-themed magazine.
8:30 a.m.	Walk short distance to office.
9:00 a.m.	Work as IT director for a medium-sized law firm.
5:00 p.m.	Clock out and head to the train station.

5:30 p.m.	Grab train and do some research on the wine industry. Update personal wine blog on favorite pick of the week.
7:00 p.m.	Arrive home and have a late dinner with the wife.
8:00 p.m.	Unwind by reading current issue of favorite wine magazine with a glass of wine. Take down some notes on blog ideas.
10:00 p.m.	Watch television.
11:00 p.m.	Head to bed.

Scenario B: Full-time online news editor, stay-at-home mom, and part-time freelance writer

6:30 a.m.	Roll out of bed, get children ready to walk to the bus stop for school, and kiss husband goodbye.
7:30 a.m.	Make coffee and feed pets. Grab a granola bar for breakfast.
8:30 a.m.	Check and respond to email, tweet, and update Facebook status for online news editing job.
9:00 a.m.	Take shower and get dressed.
9:30 a.m.	Meet local economic development coordinator for coffee and to discuss her upcoming run for state representative.
11:00 a.m.	Head home to edit stories submitted by freelance writers, respond to emails, tweet and update Facebook status.
12:30 p.m.	Take the dog for a walk.
1:00 p.m.	Grab lunch at desk while writing up story on local person running for state office using notes from morning coffee meeting. Schedule story to run later in the day.
2:00 p.m.	Head to meeting with boss and other editors to discuss this year's goals.
4:00 p.m.	Pick up children at the bus stop on the way home, make dinner, help kids with homework, and have dinner with family.
6:30 p.m.	Check email, tweet and update Facebook status while kids play.

7:00 p.m.	Help children with baths and pick out school outfits for next day.
7:30 p.m.	Head to PTO meeting after leaving husband bedtime instructions.
9:00 p.m.	Change for bed and settle back in at home. Check email, tweet, and update Facebook status. Schedule freelance stories for following day.
10:00 p.m.	Grab a glass of wine and work on freelance writer magazine articles due next week.
12:00 p.m.	Head to bed.

CASE STUDY: WRITER WITH A DAY JOB, LOOKING TO MAKE IT FULL TIME

Kathleen M. Bishop
Owner/Operator
Thru Rose Colored Glasses
6054 Stokes-Lee Center Rd.
Lee Center, NY 13363
bisburl@earthlink.net

"Writing is essentially my life or at least my therapy."

Kathleen Bishop, Ph.D.

Kathleen Bishop has been writing professionally for ten years but has been writing her entire life. She considers herself somewhere between just getting started and an expert in the field. She started writing stories and journals as a very young child and "have never stopped." Kathleen has been able to use her Ph.D. in aging and disabilities, combined with her life work and experiences, as a stepping-stone from which to build her professional writing. She has written everything from college papers, magazine, and newspaper articles to business materials, newsletters/fliers, and even books. Kathleen keeps a personal journal and has reviewed journal articles in gerontology as a professional peer.

Some of Kathleen's writing projects have included articles for monthly magazines on older women's issues, newsletters for employers, manuals for her consulting work, literally thousands of presentations, professional journal articles, and books "for herself." She currently has one published book titled *Whistling up the Wind* and is working on at least two others.

Fitting writing into her busy schedule sometimes can be a difficult task. To ensure that she writes on a regular basis, Kathleen tries to "commit to a minimum of 15 minutes to 30 minutes every day, usually just before bed." Sometimes, she is able to spend more time writing when she takes a break from working. "I am trying to be very disciplined about it, or otherwise I go lengths of time without writing for me," she said.

Kathleen has been paid for her writing in addition to donating her writing services. "I have sold books and been paid for presentations around my writing. They are usually very small stipends. Even my professional journal writing is in addition to the other work I do. Because I love to write, I have had employers who make writing part of my job, such as producing a human rights newsletter or writing on women's issues. I have written for a monthly journal for no pay."

Kathleen does not spend a lot of time searching for writing jobs. "Other than selling my books," she says, "they usually come to me." In her geographical area, she is known for presenting and writing on aging and disabilities as well as on women's history and issues. "I have spent absolutely no time doing job searching in writing, but I would love to learn how so I can make my writing my day job."

Kathleen recommends becoming an expert at something you love to help find writing jobs. For her, it has been women's issues and history. "That has led me to meet all kinds of wonderful people who ask me to do small jobs for them. Many times, though, it is voluntary. But, it is about who you meet and know."

Be open to changes in your career direction from where you thought you were going and to new directions, she advises. "Be ready to flow with new opportunities. But, first and foremost, love what you do and be passionate about it. That will bring the positive energy to you. If you are just ho hum about what you do, then those around you will react the same way to you."

The best advice Kathleen has received lately on writing is that "writers write." Just get started and do it, she suggests. "Be ready to learn from others, but write what it is you care about. If you do write for others because you need the pay, find ways to make each word satisfying. Picture the reader and the difference it could make it someone's life. Some of us are meant to be teachers and writers. If that is you, then do it!"

Kathleen currently has a website that she is in the process of revamping as the result of a recent writer's retreat. "I have reenergized myself around the website," she says, and "have hired a consultant to add sections to it including a page for women's history and what we can learn today from that history."

She plans to include links to other women's products, books, and websites when they reflect the same goals as hers as well as including a book club and a newsletter. "I am really excited about the possibilities and need to figure out how to make this pay for me so I can quit at least one of my day jobs," she said. Kathleen has committed to leaving the most time consuming and least satisfying job by December 2012 in hopes of pursuing writing on a full-time basis. She also plans to develop an active Facebook page around women's history and her writing.

Kathleen's favorite aspect of writing is the joy it gives her when she "gets a story down on paper that may help someone else or just bring pleasure to someone else." She also loves "when someone has read something I wrote and it made a difference; they understood the message."

In closing Kathleen says that writing "is very inexpensive therapy, much cheaper than the hourly rate for a professional therapist."

Life-Work Balance

Successful freelance writers, whether working at their crafts on a part-time or a full-time basis, are able to create a balance between work and personal lives. Somehow, as a society, we have long put our work life ahead of our personal lives, which causes a great imbalance. In order to create harmony, we must discover a way to balance our work with our personal lives in a way that works for us. What that means to one person might mean something different to another.

The word balance connotes that we are trying to equalize the varying sides. That lends to the thought process that our work must be in equal balance to our personal pursuits, a 50-50 division between work and play. The secret, however, is discovering the right "balance" that works for you. As shown in the examples in the previous sections on being a freelance writer on a full- or

part-time basis, we can see that a typical day is not always split equally between work and other pursuits.

Freelancers, as part of the nature of the job, have the flexibility to create the balance that works for them. If, for example, you spent an hour and a half commuting to your job two cities away, it would prove difficult to take a break and plant some veggies in your backyard garden. As a full-time freelance writer, you would be able to take that break in-between projects and sow your garden. In the case of a part-time freelance writer, you can make the commitment to pursue writing as a creative outlet during your non-day-job hours to help balance the rigidness of how you must spend your days.

Because freelance writers work from home, they can set their own schedules and can create a life-work balance that works for them. *Additional details on creating a good work schedule can be found in Chapter 4.* In order to determine what your work-life balance might mean to you, take some time to reflect. Busy successful people "find the time" to make it work, not by adding to their commitments, but by evaluating and making decisions. Often, they add, modify, delete, and prioritize what they spend the time they do have on.

In order to get everything done, you have to be able to organize and control your workload. Whether you are working as a full-time freelance writer or are trying to pursue it as a part-time venture, the following exercise will help you sort out your ideal balance:

Start by making a list of everything on your plate. A typical list might look like this:

1. Household duties (laundry, cooking, cleaning, etc.)
2. Full-time day job
3. Taking care of the kids
4. Spending time with husband
5. Pursuing a freelance writing career

6. Volunteering at church
7. Keeping in touch with friends

Look at your list and prioritize the items by order of where you spend the most of your time. A sample list of where you spend the most time might look like this:

1. Full-time day job
2. Household duties
3. Taking care of the kids
4. Volunteering at church
5. Spending time with husband
6. Pursuing a freelance writing career
7. Keeping in touch with friends

Now, look at your list and prioritize the items by order of where you would love to allot most of your time. It is OK to group items together if you need to. A sample priority list might look like this:

1. Kids and husband
2. Pursuing a writing career
3. Keeping in touch with friends
4. Volunteering at church
5. Household duties and full-time day job

Compare your lists. How do they differ? What can you do to create the work-life balance you really want?

Being a Freelancing Parent

One of the greatest challenges when working on a freelance career with small children underfoot is balancing your workload with the needs of your family. No matter how many hours or days you set aside for work, you still need to be able to cram it all into a small amount of time while the kids are napping, at school, or even at day care. A helpful solution? Grouping.

When you only have a small amount of time to get work done, it helps to be able to group tasks together. For example, when scheduling phone interviews, do so during the same time window each week. That way, you can schedule as many interviews as possible during the hours of 9 to 11:30 a.m. on Thursdays when your son is at preschool. This will make your work less "scattered" and in essence, much more productive.

Do you work on a couple of weekly columns? Group them together and set aside one day per week to work on those. It might be something like Monday nights after the kids are in bed from 8 p.m. to 10 p.m. to get those done with a quick review on Tuesday morning before the kids are up before sending them off.

Chores around the house even can be grouped together to make that aspect of your workload a little lighter. For example, Saturday afternoons after the sporting events might become your time to get your meals prepared for the week. Do all of your cooking and prep work (with the help of a little chef, if you have one) done on Saturday so meals during the week become as easy as warming up the casserole in the oven while you help the kids do homework or play a board game with them.

Some other helpful tips include:

- Get up: When every minute counts between balancing kids, work and the household, getting up a little early can add minutes and even hours to your workday. The early morning hours can be time to start that exercise routine, make lunches, throw in a load of laundry, or write that article and send off some email or Tweets. Perhaps, it could be just a few minutes to enjoy a quiet cup of coffee while setting your intentions for the day and gathering your thoughts.

- Stay up: If you are anything like me, "early morning" falls into the category of a dirty word. Instead, I find my "extra" time after the kids are in bed. Instead of sitting mindlessly in front of the television, nights have become my working hours. I kiss the little ones goodnight, make myself a cup of my favorite tea, and turn on my laptop. I write articles, I review my schedule for the next few days, I respond to email, I do research, I edit other people's writing, and I search for new jobs. Sometimes, that cup of tea is even a nice glass of wine. Because I do not get up early in the morning, I can balance the later nights so I am not feeling tired the next day.

- Schedule housework: No one actually "likes" doing housework. In my house, housework is at the bottom of my growing list of things to do. In order for it all to get done, I have started to schedule in housework times. On Mondays, Wednesdays, and Fridays, for example, I do laundry. Nightly, my husband and I are making an effort to clean off the kitchen island, where all of the papers and other miscellaneous items from the day seem to collect. On Saturday mornings, we change bed sheets, pick up the kids' rooms, and vacuum. Practice does make perfect.

- Get the family involved: Two Sundays a month, the entire family gets involved in the grocery shopping process. We cut coupons, make our lists, and head to the grocery store as a family outing. At the store, we divide and conquer. I take one of our children with half the list and my husband takes our other child with the other half of the list. We come together at the checkout line and reward ourselves with an ice cream cone or a treat at our favorite coffee / hot chocolate shop. Sometimes, we even treat ourselves to dinner. When we get home, the kids help unload the groceries and put them away.

Balancing the demands of parenthood, housework, and freelancing can be a real juggling act. If you set aside some time to figure out how you can find some "extra" time in your day and how you can group certain activities together, you can become more efficient and have more time for everything you want to get done.

To Quit or Not to Quit Your Day Job

Working full time from home as a freelance writer can be a re-warding career. It also can be scary to take the jump to get there. Taking the leap and quitting your day job to pursue writing on a full-time basis might not be for everyone. On the other hand, sometimes we are forced into starting something new when we suddenly find ourselves unemployed due to a downturn in the economy. This would be the perfect time to try writing on a full-time basis. In other cases, starting a freelance writing career might happen when you decide to leave the corporate world to stay home when your children are small. Or, perhaps, the kids have gone off to college, and you suddenly are finding yourself with more free time on your hands.

Wherever you might be in your process of becoming a freelance writer, to quit or not to quit your day job is a big decision. Many personal factors go into making the choice; there is not one right answer for everyone. Only you can determine what is best for your unique situation. In some cases, switching jobs to one that is less demanding might be in order instead of quitting completely. Or, saving up a year's worth of expenses while you keep your day job might be the right path for you before embarking on freelance writing full time.

Some things to consider when making a decision to quit your day job include:

1. **Your bottom line.** In other words, what do you need to earn in a year to effectively pay all of your bills? Do you have a mortgage? What do you spend monthly on food? Do you have a car payment? Are you in debt? What do you owe to credit card companies? If you do not already have a monthly budget, now would be the optimal time to make one. Knowing what you need to bring into the house money-wise will help you determine if you can afford to quit your day job, take on a less demanding job that frees up time to work on your writing career, or if you should keep your job to pay down debt and save money to take the plunge in a year or so. Perhaps, you need to consolidate debt to pay it down before leaving your day job permanently.

2. **Health Insurance.** One of the downsides of quitting your full-time day job might include the loss of employer-subsidized health care. There are options for buying into health-care plans as an individual or freelancer, but these numbers will need to be factored into your bottom line budgeting. Do your research. Find out what your costs are now while employed and compare it with what it would

cost you to go onto a spouse's insurance or buy into a group plan with other freelancers.

3. **Time Commitments.** When considering writing as a career, what are your time commitments? Is your full-time job your only major time constraint? How much time does your day job take up? Are you currently working part time in addition to your full-time job? Would you be able to quit one of those jobs to pursue writing during the time that job was previously taking up? Are you able to spend time working on your writing while keeping your full-time job? Perhaps, taking on a part-time job instead of a full time job would provide you with enough money to live while allotting more time to pursue your writing dreams. Refer to the work-life balance lists you created in the previous section. Besides your job, what other time commitments do you have?

Here are some tips and suggestions to help you figure out whether quitting your day job is the best option for you:

1. Create an honest budget.

   - Start by listing all of your fixed expenses. Examples might include rent/mortgage, electricity, oil, car payment, car insurance, etc.
   - What do you spend on groceries in a month? What about gas for the car?
   - Do you have credit-card debt? Are you paying it back on a monthly basis?

- Do you have a latte habit? Or eat out often? Do not forget to include incidentals like these, as they can really add up.
- Multiply the above items by 12 to figure out approximately what you might spend in a year on expenses.
- What about once-a-year expenses such as vacations, car registrations, and magazine subscriptions? Add these to your yearly numbers.
- Are you willing to trim your expenses to pursue writing on a full-time basis?

2. Do you contribute to a savings account on a monthly basis? Do you have enough saved up to pay for a year's worth of expenses while you get your freelance writing business going?

3. Make a list of the pros and cons of your current day job. Items might include benefits such as health insurance or a paycheck that covers the mortgage. Disadvantages could be that it does not allow you enough time to pursue other interests.

4. Determine what your life would look like if you quit your day job.

- Would you have enough money to pay your bills?
- Would it free up enough time to work on writing as a full-time endeavor?
- Would expenses change if you quit your job? For example, would you spend less gas money on

commuting, buying lunch out, or other work-related expenses, such as clothes for the office?

- How do you think you would spend your days?
- Do you have all the tools you need to get started on writing? Or do you need to save up to purchase a laptop?
- Would it be better to look for a part-time job instead?

A quick budget worksheet might look something like this:

EXPENSES	Monthly	Yearly
Rent	700	
Car Payment	199	
Electricity	100	
Gas	200	
Groceries	400	
Daily Coffee	100	
Vacation		2000
Car Insurance		800
Clothes for work		300
TOTAL	1699	3100
	x 12 months	
	20, 388	

In this simplified example, total yearly expenses would be $23,488.

Many free budgeting templates are available online to help you with this process. Just type in "free budget worksheet" in your Web browser's search bar to find one that fits your needs.

Example: Day job pros vs. cons
Job: Office worker

PROS	CONS
Regular paycheck that covers all expenses	Long commute
Health insurance	Work more than 40 hours for no additional pay
401K	Not creative
Company-provided laptop	Not appreciated
Company-provided cell phone	Frustrating/not rewarding
	No extra time to pursue other interests

Do the pros outweigh the cons?

CASE STUDY:
TAKING TIME OFF

Chrissy Lewis
4737 Golfview Drive
Roanoke,VA 24019
Chlewis_2@yahoo.com

"I took six months off to really take a good, hard look at what I wanted to do with my life."

Chrissy Lewis is a social worker with a B.A. in clinical psychology and an M.A. in counseling. She is just getting started as a writer and has taken a few months off from work to pursue the possibly of writing. She has experience writing college papers and keeps a journal. Additionally, she has begun writing a book.

"My actual writing experiences are limited at this point," she says, "but I have written down quite a few notes on one story, and I have started typing up another story that has taken shape right before my eyes!"

"Initially after working a job I came to hate," she says, "I took six months off to really take a good, hard look at what I wanted to do with my life."

After some soul searching, Chrissy came to the realization that her love of reading that began in childhood, coupled with ideas that she had been forming, could be channeled into a writing career. "The realization felt so good, it released a swirl of butterflies in my stomach!"

Chrissy says she has had to work through "many fears, self doubts, sabotaging behaviors and excuses" to really start writing and commit to it.

"The process was worth it and having others read my work and like it is such a joy it pushes me to keep writing."

Currently, Chrissy sets aside at least two hours to write every evening and tries to fit in four hours of writing on Saturdays and Sundays, when possible.

Chrissy enjoys being able to let the creative juices flow. "I love creating stories and characters from ideas in my mind and then shaping it all into a story. I also love seeing the story take shape, sometimes going places I had not anticipated.

"It's a fun and amazing process," she says, "I get to set my pace and my schedule — it's a freedom like no other."

To other aspiring writers, Chrissy says "Just start writing, whatever it is. Don't edit yourself, just get in a groove where you are comfortable with the pace and you can get your thoughts on paper."

She suggests surrounding yourself with other writers by attending workshops, retreats, meetings, groups… "whatever to get the writer inside you inspired and supported.

"If you want to write, just write," she says.

"Write something everyday. Trust that the inherent desire to write means something and that the tools, support, information, etc., will come to you.

"Try to remain positive and think of all the people who have come to greatness-if they can do it, so can you."

Unless you have six months to one year's worth of living expenses stored away in a high-yielding saving account, I would highly recommend stepping slowly into freelance writing. Keeping a part time or other flexible day job while you collect as many clients, portfolio pieces, and other contacts as you can is the ideal way to get a leg up on quitting your day job. By taking advantage of a steady paycheck, you can stockpile some cash to get through the transition to full-time freelance writer.

If you have a traditional 9-to-5 job, you may want to trade that in for a more flexible position that offers mornings or an extra day off a week to commit to your writing endeavors. Otherwise, you may have to work freelance writing into odd times like the wee hours of the morning or late into the night after the kids are asleep.

If you recently have lost your job or are a stay-at-home parent, you already may have the "extra" time to work at becoming a successful freelance writer while the kids are in school. If you do decide to quit a day job, on the other hand, you might want to consider taking on part-time jobs or temporary jobs to fill in the gaps while you are building your full-time writing business.

Becoming a freelance writer requires work on your part; it is not as easy as waking up one day, quitting your job, and immediately selling your work at top dollar to clients who come knocking on your door. It is a labor of love and perseverance. No matter where you might be in your writing journey, you will need to do your homework. Figuring out if you should keep your day job is just one piece to the puzzle of becoming a freelance writer. Writing often and learning the basics of the writing business is next.

What is a Successful Freelance Writer?

Success is subjective. Often, it is in the eye of the beholder, whether it is your eye or someone looking in from the outside. For most freelance writers, success might be measured as being able to support a family financially, while working at a personally fulfilling career with a flexible work schedule. For others, it might be something along the lines of having a byline in a well-known magazine. Others still might find success in a large paycheck as validation for all of their hard work.

Take some time to think about what being a successful freelance writer might mean to you. If you are living your own version of success, or taking the necessary steps to get there, you should not worry what other people think. You should be proud of what success means for you and just go for it

Author's Note

For me, I think success as a freelance writer means that I can enjoy a personally fulfilling career that brings in a decent paycheck and allots me the time I need to spend with my family. Success is being able to have a happy work-life balance that includes a fun and flexible job, while working it around the needs of my family. Having a good paycheck just adds to being able to do things with my family, such as travel. Although, I will admit, seeing my name in print in a magazine or online is an incredible experience!

Chapter 2

READY, SET....WRITE

"Keep away from people who try to belittle your ambitions. Small people always do that, but the really great make you feel that you, too, can become great."

— Mark Twain, author and humorist

Understanding the process and mechanics of writing is a crucial step to becoming a successful freelance writer. So is finding the time to write every day. *This will be discussed further in Chapter 4.* Knowing your personal writing style, assessing your strengths and weaknesses, and being able to adapt your writing will allow you the flexibility to take on a variety of writing projects for a wide range of clients.

A good writer also has knowledge of the basics of writing. Good grammar, spelling, and punctuation skills are paramount to the business and key in getting writing jobs. Being familiar with various writing styles (APA, Chicago, etc.) also will make you more marketable. Another valuable skill for a writer to possess is how to work with an editor. Writing is a craft, and learning to hone your craft will help you in becoming a successful writer.

CASE STUDY: DEVELOPING THE CRAFT OF WRITING

J.C. Cobb
PO Box 814
Pinetops, NC 27864
coachjcobb@gmail.com

"Writing is a craft that needs development." J.C. Cobb

J.C. Cobb has been writing recreationally for about ten years and as a professional for the past year. J.C. has a bachelor's degree in English (creative writing) and a master's degree in education, and he considers his writing experience just past that of someone getting started. He has written college papers, magazine and newspaper articles, poetry, business materials, online articles, newsletters/fliers, and anthology excerpts. Additionally, he keeps a personal journal.

J.C. began writing when he was in high school. He wrote song lyrics to accompany compositions on his guitar. Song lyrics, in turn, led to a "fascination with narratives and poetry" and played into to his lifelong love of words. J.C.'s favorite aspect of writing is "the opportunity to impart an important truth to the reader." He loves "words that inspire, stories that are infused with life- altering characters and paradigms; shifting ideas."

Writing is currently a "side project" to J.C.'s full-time job of English teacher and coach. He has been published in local newspapers and magazines and currently is working on a project compiling the history of his Masonic lodge in a self-published book. He also has worked on an anthology of Edgecombe County and has edited the writings of local professionals. J.C. also dabbles in writing fiction, poetry, and song lyrics.

J.C. used to fit writing into his schedule when he could, but now he is making more of an effort to schedule writing time on a regular basis. Every night at 9:30 p.m., he commits to a minimum of 15 minutes of writing time, sometimes writing for up to three hours. J.C. takes on writing projects that he wants to work on for personal reasons, along with those that he has been asked to write for others.

To writers just starting out, he suggests they "write anything you can and send it to local newspapers and magazines to get your name out locally." Writing is a craft, he says, that needs to be developed. First, "read, read, read, and read some more. Writers must be knowledgeable in all things and pay attention to the way other writers write. Second, identify the style and prose of other writers you would like to emulate."

Then, he says, you need to practice daily by "creating characters and situations that enable you to develop your own distinct voice on the page." When you write something you think to be outstanding, J.C. suggests you hide it from yourself for "at least two weeks." After time has passed, "revisit your writing and see if you still feel the same way about it."

Discover Your Personal Writing Style

Anyone can learn the mechanics of writing, like spelling and grammar. Discovering your writing style, however, is a personal journey, one filled with a uniqueness that is all your own. Where your grew up, how your live, your past jobs, your family, your relationships, your experiences in school, etc., all contribute to the person you are today. All those things also reflect through your writing.

Are you a meticulous grammar-nut? Do you know the basics of writing but enjoy starting sentences with prepositional words like "and" or "because"? Do you naturally write in narrative form? Do you find yourself writing in a top-down journalistic style and just cover the facts? These things all play into your personal writing style. Knowing and understanding your personal writing style will help you adjust your writing to your clients needs and be able to edit yourself for publication.

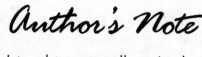

Author's Note

I tend to naturally write long, drawn-out sentences with lots of descriptive details. When writing for newspapers, however, I have to be careful of my writing style by remembering to keep my sentences simple, straightforward, and just about the facts. My natural style, on the other hand, tends to be well suited for feature-style magazine articles where flowery, descriptive sentences help paint the picture that tells the story.

Knowing your personal writing style will help you become a better writer. Figuring out your strengths, weaknesses, and other nuances will help you take better advantage of your individual talents and expand the impact of your writing. It also will help you determine what markets would fit your writing style best. This does not mean, however, that you should only write where you are comfortable. Stretching your skills and playing with different styles will only help you become more marketable as a freelance writer.

However, in stretching yourself, remember to work within your own style. If you try to "copy" someone else's personal style, you will only be doing a disservice to yourself, as you will find great difficulty emulating someone else. Your work, in this case, will not come across as authentic.

The number of personal writing styles varies greatly. Each writer brings his or her own uniqueness to the table when writing. Some basic writing styles might include the following:

Unbiased Observer: People who write in this type of style use smaller words and shorter sentences. A broad, general audience easily understands this style of writing. It is fact-based, organized, and concise. It is also free of bias, opinions, and emotions. This style of writing is suitable for journalism, reviews, news reporting, scientific documents, legal papers, or technical writing.

Emotionally Reactive: This style of writing is emotional and opinionated. It is used as way to express anger, fear, grief, or joy about a topic. The writing often includes a heavy use of the word "I" as opposed to the unbiased observer who never/rarely uses the word "I." This style of writing is ideal for editorials, opinion articles, blogs, or reviews. Writers who are emotionally reactive often invoke controversial responses to their work.

Poetic: Writers who like to convey dreams, thoughts, emotions, or observations in a structured writing form such as poetry or prose fall into this category. This style writer views writing as an art form, revising and rewriting their work until it is crafted into the perfect piece of "words as art." This writer loves to use metaphors, write in a rhythmic fashion, and play with sentence and word structures.

Story weaver: This narrative writing style is designed to entertain the reader. The writing is done in story-form and includes colorful character descriptions, details of places, and a series of events. The story weaver writes about emotions, feelings, and experiences to allow the reader to be an active observer in the story. This style of writing can be fictional or nonfictional.

Expert: This writer writes basic how-to, nonfiction pieces. He or she is knowledgeable about a specific topic or is a master of a skill he or she wants to teach. These writers write about what they are experts at and often research new things to teach others about through their writing. Technical papers, medical essays, legal studies, and academic writings fall into this category.

Do any of these categories describe your writing style? Are you a combination of two or more of these or something different?

No matter what your personal writing style is, you easily can adapt your writing to fit into any medium.

Figure out Your Personal Writing Style

To help you figure out which style, or combination of styles you fit into, try this exercise.

1. Take the facts below and write a story using them. You can use some or all of the facts. You can stick to "just the facts" or add in any additional details you can create or research to complete the story the way you think it should be written.

2. Give yourself a time limit of 30 to 45 minutes to complete this task without distraction.

3. Do not think too much about it and do not edit yourself as you go, just write to allow your natural style to shine through.

4. After you are done, see if your "style" fits into the ones described in this chapter. Is there one style you lean toward? How can you use your style to your advantage? Is there a specific market that your writing might be suited for?

FACTS:

- The Alves family decides to plant a vineyard.

- There are four members of their immediate family: a mother, a father, a 7-year-old daughter, and a 4-year-old boy.

- They plan to do so on five acres of property in their backyard in the Northeastern part of the United States.

- They have chosen four varieties of grapes to plant.

- Their ultimate goal is to create a vineyard where they produce and sell their own brand of wine.

Adapting Your Writing Style to Suit Any Medium

As a freelance writer, you will need to be able to alter your style to suit the job. This encompasses not only grammatical style, but also having the ability to match your writing to the subject matter and writing platform. For example, feature writing is different from Web content, and news reporting is distinctly different from academic writing. Writers have the ability to influence, inform, and inspire readers, but only if you can effectively use your words to get your point across.

Before pitching your ideas to a specific publication, it is a good idea to research and understand the needs of that specific publication. What style do they publish? Do they follow a specific style format? Are their stories more fact-based? More fictionalized? *For more details on targeting your submissions, see Chapter 7.*

Keys to Being Able to Adapt Your Writing Style:

1. Know what your personal writing style is. If you can dissect your own style, it will be easier to adjust your writing to be more suitable for other platforms.

2. Understand the different types of writing styles and the requirements for each platform. For example, what works on the Web might not work in your favorite magazine.

3. Identify the style of the client you are writing for and try to write in their "voice." Make sure you tailor your style to fit what they are looking for while still letting a little of you seep through.

The ability to diversify only will aid in making you that much more marketable as a freelance writer. Successful writers continually hone their skill and style through research and practice. Learning the ins and outs of various writing styles will help ensure your ability to earn a variety of jobs to keep the paychecks coming in. If you do not know the difference in style from a press release and a blog, it will be difficult to get your writing business off the ground. It is not the job of the client to dictate style, it is your responsibility to research and learn the various styles and tailor yourself to suit their needs.

More details will be included in later chapters, but some basic styles are:

Newspaper: Newspaper articles, especially hard news style stories, are written in an inverted pyramid style. What this means is that all the basic facts come first, and as you move through the story, additional details and background information is filtered in. Writers who write for newspapers consider the following:

- Include all the basic facts of who, what, when, where, and why at the top of the story. This is also known as answering the five W's.

- The five W's are then followed by important details with general information and background details closing out the end.

- Journalistic prose is precise and does not use jargon or contractions.

- Newspaper writers will use short, concise words that are easily understood by the masses.

- News writers avoid repeating the same word more than once in a paragraph.

- Simple subject-verb sentence structures are used.

Online writing: Writing for an online audience requires that you get the most "bang for your buck." Online readers move on quickly and need easy-to-read content that tells the basics up front. Some basic tips for writing online include:

- Keep it simple. When writing online, your target audience members are "scanners" not readers. Ensure information is clear and concise.

- Keep paragraphs short.

- Consider how the copy will look on a Web page. Unlike full-page size, online copy is often broken up into shorter blocks.

- Think like a journalist (see previous section).

- Consider SEO (search engine optimization) and use descriptive titles that will get picked up by search engines. More on SEO will be discussed in a later chapter. For example, what would you type into a search bar if you were looking for information on a particular topic?

- Break it up. Chop up long sentences; simplify word choice. Online articles reach a wider audience that might not know the language as well as you do.

- Use links. Not all the information online is collected on the same page. Links are a way to break up information in a simpler manner. *More information on links will be discussed in Chapter 7.*

Business: To write for business, you must write in a clear, concise manner. Being able to convey information that is easily discernable and quickly understood whether it is a presentation, brochure, Web page content, or white paper is the key to being a successful business writer. Some tips when writing for business include:

- Be organized
- Keep your audience in mind
- Proofread
- Edit yourself

These tips also apply to other writing as well.

The Importance of Grammar and Spelling

In addition to style, grammar and spelling go a long way when trying to land writing jobs.

Writers write, but good writers know how to write. Effective writing not only depends on content but also on clarity and readability. A challenge all writers face is choosing just the right words to craft good sentences while expressing your thoughts in a clear, concise, and interesting manner. Some key factors in effective writing include proper organization and development of your ideas and overall coherence of your work, along with the writer's command of grammar and sentence structure. This is not to mention the mechanics of writing like capitalization, punctuation, and spelling, etc.

Understanding the basic rules of grammar is paramount not only when writing a piece for a client but also in being able to get a job. Would you hire a car mechanic who does not know a basic task like changing a flat tire? Likewise, to make it as a successful freelance writer, it is important to understand some basic grammar rules.

Grammar Resources

Hundreds of grammar reference books are on the market, as well as a host of Internet resources if you want a more in-depth look at grammar rules, but it is best to find one or two good references to have on hand. Some good ones are:

- *Eats, Shoots & Leaves: The Zero Tolerance Approach to Punctuation*, Lynne Truss (Gotham, 2006)

- *The Elements of Style*, William Strunk (Longman, 1999)

- *Woe is I: The Grammarphobe's Guide to Better English in Plain English*, Patricia T. O'Connor (Riverhead Trade, 2010)

Do not forget a good dictionary and thesaurus are must-haves. Luckily, with the Web, hundreds if not thousands of online resources are available. Be sure to find a reliable online source, however.

Here are the basics to get you started.

Spelling

Spelling is an important part of writing. It is key in presenting yourself as a professional writer. Not only does your copy need to be error free, but also so should all your correspondence with the client. Inaccurate spelling will confuse the message and downgrade the quality of your work. Without proper spelling, humans cannot communicate effectively with each other.

Grammar and Spelling Check Programs

In addition to understanding the basic rules of grammar, grammar and spell-check options are built into most programs. The danger, however, comes when relying solely on those features. A computer, for example, will not make a distinction between "your" and "you're" or "their" and "there." It also will not tell you if you accidentally type the wrong word, such as typing "food" when you mean "good." This is why knowing the basics are key, and you should use the built-in checks only as a backup.

Commas, semicolons, and colons, oh my!

Punctuation is key in ensuring what you intended to say is what you actually said. Knowing the rules and using punctuation properly will affect the quality of your work. The *Chicago Manual of Style*, for example, gives 16 pages worth of comma usage instruction. Luckily, you will not need to memorize *all* the various styles out there, but it is important to know the basics and have the various style guides on hand for quick reference.

For example, look at these sentences that change meaning with a mere comma placement:

- Slow, children crossing. (Go slow because children are crossing)
  Slow children crossing. (Slow children are crossing)
- Let's eat, Grandma (It is time to eat, Grandma.)
  Let's eat Grandma. (We are cooking our Grandma for dinner.)

There are countless style rules for comma usage, and each depends on the style guide you are using. *You will learn more about style guides in the following sections.* In general, eight basic rules are as follows:

1. Use a comma when noting dates and addresses.
   - *Today is April 1, 2012.*
2. Use commas to separate three or more words or phrases in a series.
   - *I packed flip-flops, towels, and a bathing suit for my trip to the beach.*
   - *The students exhibited patience, good judgment, and perseverance when working together to get the project done.*

NOTE: A debate rages amongst various styles about placing a comma before the "and." It is often referred to as the "Oxford comma" or the "serial comma." Many style guides make use of the serial comma, yet when writing for a newspaper publication that follows AP Style, the comma before the conjunction is eliminated. For example, *Melissa got an "A" in anatomy, business and body systems.*

3. Use commas to indicate that a person is being addressed by name.
   - *Georgina, did you make this pretty dress?*
   - *Did you make this pretty dress, Georgina?*
4. Use commas after phrases, clauses, or small words that introduce the main idea of your sentence.
   - *No, David did not take his medicine today.*
   - *After dinner, we all went out to see a movie.*
   - *On the other hand, we did get to meet the band after the concert.*

- *During the night, they heard many owls hooting in the distance.*

5. Use commas to set off words, phrases, or clauses that give additional information about the main part of the sentence or otherwise interrupt the natural flow of the sentence.

    - *Shannon, my cousin, lives in Rhode Island.*
    - *Amy, after finishing nursing school, got a job working at the hospital.*
    - *Andrew, in the meantime, starting designing Web pages.*

6. Use a comma between coordinate adjectives not joined by "and."

    - *The trip they went on was a sacred, spiritual adventure in France.* (sacred and spiritual both modify adventure)
    - But, NOT in this case: *The group all wore matching bright green shirts.* (bright modifies green and matching modifies shirts so the adjectives are not "coordinate")

7. Use a comma before nonessential, modifying elements that follow the words and main clause and provide information that supplements the basic meaning of the main clause.

    - Many writers struggle with the nuances of grammar, of which there are many.
    - We are looking to buy a home in France, the land of "laid-back living."

8. Use commas before coordinating conjunctions such as "and," "or," or "but" that join two complete sentences or when the comma is needed for clarity, emphasis, or contrast.

    - The Connecticut River may be far away, but it is a great place to visit.

- Chauncey started skydiving, and he has become more confident because of it.
- Chantal decided to paint the canvas red, or she may paint it orange instead.

Now that you have commas down, what do you do with semicolons? The semicolon is a fun little punctuation mark avoided by most people because they are not sure when to use it. Other writers, on the other hand, love semicolons, and when used properly, they can really emphasize your point. You would use a semicolon in a couple of places:

1. To separate consecutive independent clauses when there is no coordinating conjunction between them and you do not want to use a period
   - *What an amazing opportunity; you must be so excited!*
2. To separate items in a list of three or more if any of the items has a comma, as with a nonrestrictive element
   - *They plan to study French, for their travels; Latin, for their schoolwork; and Portuguese, for their own enjoyment.*

Like the semicolon, a colon has two main uses:

1. To provide additional details and explanation
   - *In this book, I am providing usage examples for the following: commas, semicolons, and colons.*
2. To introduce a direct quote (a comma can also be used in this type of situation)
   - Joyce said to Anastasia: "I cannot believe how lucky we are!

Watch your tenses

Tense locates a situation in time, to indicate when the situation takes place; the basic tenses are past, present, and future. Using the proper tense in writing is important. Tense refers to the form of the verb that indicates time. A change in tense helps locate the timing of the story for a reader. Changing the tense too often will confuse the reader. All events that happen within the same time should all have the same verb tense. Tenses are powerful in writing and can change the entire meaning of the sentence if not used properly. The basic tenses are as follows:

- **Present:** The present tense indicates that an action is present, now, relative to the speaker or writer.

- **Past:** The past tense indicates that the action is in the past, relative to the speaker or writer.

- **Future:** The future tense indicates that the action will happen in the future, relative to the speaker or writer.

When writing, it is important to pay attention to tenses. Here is a chart on all of the various forms of tenses and proper usage:

Tense	Definition	Use
Present Simple	The simple present expresses an action in the present taking place once, never, or several times.	• She dances. • Does she sing?
Present Progressive	The present progressive is used for actions going on in the moment of speaking and for actions taking place only for a short period.	• She is dancing. • Is she singing?

Tense	Definition	Use
Present Perfect	An action that stopped recently.	• She has danced. • Has she sung?
Present Perfect Progressive	An action that recently stopped or is still going on.	• She has been dancing. • Has she been singing?
Past Simple	The simple past expresses an action in the past taking place once, never, several times.	• She danced. • Did she sing?
Past Progressive	An action **going on** at a certain time in the past.	• She was dancing. • Was she singing?
Past Perfect	An action in the past that occurred before something else, usually another event.	• She had danced. • Had she sung?
Past Perfect Progressive	An action continued in the past that occurred before something else, usually another event.	• She had been dancing. • Had she been singing?
Future Simple	An action in the future that cannot be influenced.	• She will dance. • Will she sing?
Future Progressive	An action that is **going on** at a certain time in the future.	• She will be dancing. • Will she be singing?
Future Perfect	An action that will be **finished** at a certain time in the future.	• She will have danced. • Will she have sung?
Future Perfect Progressive	An action taking place before a certain time in the future.	• She will have been dancing. • Will she have sung?
Conditional I Simple	An action that **might** take place.	• She would dance. • Would she have sung?
Conditional I Progressive	An action that might take place.	• She would be singing. • Would she be dancing?

Tense	Definition	Use
Conditional II Simple	An action that **might** have taken place in the past.	• She would have sung. • Would she have danced?
Conditional II Progressive	An action that might have taken place in the past.	• She would have been singing. • Would she have been dancing?

After reading through that chart, are you more confused than ever? A simplistic way to look at the usage of tense when writing is this: The tense you use depends on how you see the event or action. For example, when writing a news story about a fire that happened last night, the tense would be in the past because the fire had already happened. If you were on the scene writing about the fire as it was happening, however, you would use the present tense.

Common Style Manuals and What to Know About Them

A style manual, or style guide, is a handbook that dictates the acceptable style for a particular type of publication. When working as a freelance writer, you do not have to know the specific details and ins and outs of all the possible guidelines out there, but you do need to have a basic knowledge, especially if you plan to write mostly for a particular type of publication. This is where having a variety of style guides on hand will become a valuable asset. It is extremely important to know which style guide your client or editor expects you to follow. This will help both of you in creating a great product suitable to the audience you are targeting. Some common style guides are:

Associated Press or **AP Style:** AP style was developed and is maintained by the Associated Press, the world's oldest news service. This is the gold style format used for journalists and news writing. Most magazines, especially news magazines, adhere to this style. This style is plain; it keeps things like underlining and italics to a minimum if it uses them at all. The style guide is constantly being updating to reflect changing technology and industry standards. Be sure to get up-to-date information by referencing the most current edition or checking the website at **www. apstylebook.com**. They even have an online edition that is updated constantly with the newest information. The *AP Stylebook* is vast and ever evolving, but here is a sampling of what you will find in it:

- **Ages:** In AP style, ages are always expressed as numerals.

- **Numbers:** One through nine are spelled out, while 10 and above are generally written as numerals. (If a sentence begins with a number, it should be spelled out or the sentence rewritten.)

- **Street Addresses:** Numerals always are used for numbered addresses. Street, avenue, and boulevard are abbreviated when used with a numbered address, but otherwise are spelled out. Route and road are never abbreviated.

- **Dollar Amounts:** Dollar amounts always are expressed as numerals, and the "$" sign is used.

- **Percentages:** Percentages are always expressed as numerals, followed by the word "percent."

- **Dates:** Dates are expressed as numerals. The months August through February are abbreviated when used with numbered dates. March through July are never abbreviated. Months without dates are not abbreviated. "Th" is not used to express a day.

- **Job Titles:** Job titles generally are capitalized when they appear before a person's name but lowercased after the name.

And, these are just the tip of the iceberg.

Chicago Manual of Style. CMS is the standard for book publishing, both fiction and nonfiction. It generally is not used for scholarly publishing (journals and research), but it is sometimes used for history. The CMS primarily is concerned with the preparation and editing of papers and books for publication. The University of Chicago Press has published the CMS since the early 1900s. It is published in hardcover and online at **www.chicagomanualofstyle.org/home.html**. Much more dense than the *AP Stylebook*, the CMS is nearly double the size. Here are a small percentage of the basic rules you will find in it:

- **Ages:** In CMS style, ages are always spelled out.

- **Numbers:** Numbers under 100 are spelled out, 100 and above are figures.

- **Percentages:** Always use numbers and when possible, the word *percent*. In space-constrained areas like tables, the % symbol can be used instead.

- **Million, billion:** Always use figures and spell out the words *million* and *billion*.

- **Month, day:** Always spell out the month, and use figures for the day. Avoid the use of figures for the month.

- **Month, year:** If month, day, and year are present, set off the year with matching commas. Otherwise, do not use commas.

- **Time:** Use lowercase a.m. and p.m., with periods. Always use figures, with a space between the time and the a.m. or p.m. If it is an exact hour, no ":00" is required. If a time range is entirely in the morning or evening, use a.m. or p.m. only once.

- **Cities, states:** When used on their own, state names should be spelled out, yet when there is a city, the state name is abbreviated. Add in a zip code, and the two-letter form of the state abbreviation should be used.

- **Capitalization and titles:** Things such as books, movies, paintings, and are italicized in text. For individuals, capitalize a person's title only if it precedes his or her name and modified.

- **Lists:** For lists, capitalize the first word after each bullet or number and insert a period at the end of each item only if it is a complete sentence, or if the list has a mix of complete and incomplete sentences.

- **The Internet:** The words *Internet* and *Web* are capitalized.

- **URLs:** In general-purpose text, addresses are given in the same typeface as the text in which they appear.

Confused yet? As you can see by some of the differences between AP and CMS styles, the differences are subtle, but vary greatly.

The Gregg Reference Manual: This style format is widely used in business and professional circles. The Gregg Reference Manual is "intended for anyone who writes, edits, or prepares material for distribution or publication." It is available in book form as well as online at **www.mhhe.com/business/buscom/gregg**. The book is named after John Robert Gregg and published by Mac-Graw-Hill.

MLA. The Modern Language Association style is almost exclusively used in the academic world. It applies mostly to literature and the humanities. This is the style first introduced to most writing students and undergrads. It is similar to CMS. MLA Style guides are available in paper copy and include general style guidelines such as no title page and a header that lists the author's last name and the page number and in the upper right-hand corner of all pages. Other general guidelines include writing in a legible font, using a one-inch margin on all sides, and a one-half-inch indent at the beginning of paragraphs.

A Note on Working with Editors

Even though you are a freelance writer, you will be working closely with editors that may vary from project to project or from client to client. The role of an editor is to help perfect your work. An editor has the ability to examine your work through your reader's viewpoint and see all those little details you might have missed. Their job is not to pick on you or pull apart your hard work, even though it might seem like it at the time. An editor helps ensure that the work you are producing is grammatically correct, flows, and makes logical sense in telling the story. When you are writing, rereading, and rewriting something, you often make some of the simplest mistakes because you have seen it so many times. Here are some tips to working with an editor:

- **Be professional:** Editors appreciate a professional writer and look forward to working with you again if you can meet your deadlines and provide clean, well-researched copy. If you run into a problem, always let your editor (or client) know when it happens instead of waiting until the last minute. Editors, like writers, plan their schedules around expected workloads, and a late story can throw off their scheduled workweek.

- **Be a team player:** From the beginning, go into any project with the mindset that you are not just an individual working on the project, but part of a larger team. Often, a variety of people are working toward the same goal in a publication: writer, editor, graphic artist, layout manager, etc.

- **Be flexible:** Always be prepared to adjust a deadline or change the focus of a project depending on the publication you are working with. Editors remember your hard work and willingness to work as part of the team. This often translates into additional jobs.

- **Welcome rewrites:** As hard as it is to see your work marked up with an editor's commentary, it is important to be open to your editor's request for a little more time spent on tweaking your work to better suit the publication's expectations.

- **Know the calendar:** Publications often have an editorial calendar that drives story content based on the time of year. For example, the June issue in a children's magazine might focus on summer camps. This would be the ideal time to propose an article that you have been thinking about writing on how to survive sleepaway camp.

- **Stay in touch:** Publications fold, editors move on. When you have a good relationship with an editor, keep in touch when they move on. Research their new publication, and submit some ideas for possible stories.

Freelancing is a two-way street; being a partner with your editor will benefit both of you in the end. It is important to foster a good team-based working relationship with your editor. With that in mind, editors will NOT do the following:

- **Provide direction beyond the original assignment:** Which means it is key that you, as the writer, understand the assignment when it is made.

- **Hold your hand:** Editors, like writers, are busy trying to juggle multiple tasks and projects. Your editor does not want to check in daily on how you are coming along but does want to see results on your progress.

- **Let you determine the final details:** Once you have finished writing, you turn your work over to the trust of your editor to find the perfect headline, pullouts, and design. This is why working with an editor is a partnership and two-way street.

On the other hand, while being flexible, do not allow your editor to bully you. If an editor constantly moves up deadlines and expects you to reach unrealistic goals, he or she is not doing his or her part in your partnership. A freelancer should expect the following when working with an editor:

- **Good communication:** An editor should communicate to you when you can expect to see your work in print and provide you with a final copy of what the work will look like when it goes to print. An editor also should let you know if there are any changes to the status of your work, for example, if it had to be moved to another issue or shortened to fit within a certain column size.

- **Written agreements:** A written agreement should be provided that outlines the project, payment process, rights sold, and delivery mode. If you are working with a publication that does not provide you with a formal agreement, email the editor with a list of your understanding of the terms, and wait for confirmation before beginning the project.

- **Team camaraderie:** Freelancers are an important part of the team and, as such, should be treated with respect and courtesy. An editor should never berate, lie, or be abusive in any way.

Just like you would not want to work with a difficult editor, editors do not want to work with a difficult writer. Writers need to know how to respond to criticism, overcome their own professional weaknesses, and avoid alienating editors. Just as all writers are not the same, all editors are not the same. Generally, the following tendencies can rub an editor the wrong way and are worth avoiding to the extreme:

- **Being a prima donna:** As writers, we have a tendency to love our own work, especially, when we have written and rewritten several times to get it "just right." Prima donnas, however, yell and scream, whine and cajole any time a single comma is removed or a word is substituted for another. The best way to avoid falling into this category, no matter how much it might hurt when you are edited, is to realize that your editor is only doing his or her job in perfecting your writing for his or her specific publication. Respect their comments and changes, and try to view it from their perspectives. If a change is made that you have trouble with, choose your battles, and politely voice your concerns.

- **Missing deadlines without notice:** If you need to miss a deadline, contact your editors as soon as you realize you are not going to make it. Let them know why and when you expect to have it done. For writers who have proven themselves in the past by being on time, editors will accept an occasional missed deadline. Do not make a habit of it, though. It is bad form and unprofessional.

- **Not following the guidelines:** There are guidelines for a reason. Every publication has its own set of guidelines, and writing for that publication requires you stick to the guidelines and project scope. If a project calls for 500 words, do not turn in 5,000 words.

With a little bit of effort on your part, you can become the type of freelance writer most editors like to work with when developing a team.

Chapter 3

STORY IDEAS

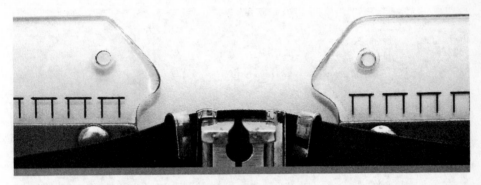

"Everybody walks past a thousand story ideas every day. The good writers are the ones who see five or six of them. Most people don't see any."

— Orson Scott Card,
author, critic, public speaker, essayist,
columnist, and political activist

You are ready to be a writer, but have no idea what to write about. However, behind every great article, story, or commentary is an idea. Behind every sentence, behind every written word, is an idea. Thinking up ideas is a skill that not every writer is born with, but it can be developed over time. Sometimes, getting started in coming up with ideas is the hardest part. After years of working as a freelance writer, you will find no end to the possible story ideas. Determining what to write is a combination of discovering what you like to write, finding out what story ideas are marketable, and formulating an idea around that.

CASE STUDY: PROFESSIONAL WRITER WITH A STYLE ALL HER OWN

Lauren E. (p/k/a "L.E.") Agnelli
Your Legacy Writer
Principal/President/Queen/
Grand High Poobah
Chester, CT
leagnelli@comcast.net or
legawriter@gmail.com
Lauren Agnelli Words and Music on
www.blogspot/blogger.com
860.526.4777

"Seriously, I kind of pity my husband or any other person around who has to live with a writer… not that I'm hard to be around or a bad person, per se, but I know I'm preoccupied, distracted, don't always listen too well, and always want to "escape" into my writing because it's safe, beautiful, and very convenient for me."

Lauren Agnelli has been writing professionally for 38 years. She has a bachelor's in creative writing and has written literally everything from college papers to magazine articles to books to business materials and everything in between. She is also a successful songwriter and musician.

"I have always written, read, kept writing, dreamed writing, wrote in school instead of paying attention, loved to write, kept writing, have been in publication for dozens of newspapers, magazines, journals, online publications, blogs, you name it," she says.

"I wrote under the pen name Trixie A. Balm when I started out doing music writing, then switched to L.E. Agnelli because I like the mysteriousness of it... I wrote (and rewrote) a novel in college and finished it for credit for my senior project... it had interest from several agents but ultimately didn't see publication (yet) but that's the only past project that hasn't seen light of day — publication, that is. I am relentless in pursuing paying gigs as a writer, and keep hoping to improve in that respect. But yes, I think I'm ready for prime time, as the saying goes."

About half of Lauren's income is generating through her writing endeavors and she spends most of her time honing her craft. "I get up, I write. I go out, I write in my head. I come home, I sit down and write again. I'm at another job, and I steal moments to write in my omnipresent spiral notebook. After dinner, I'm usually back on the computer, writing if I'm not rehearsing or doing something else that is pressing. I am not reading as much as I'd like to; instead, I'm writing."

Lauren finds most of her writing gigs through networking. "And if I had more time, I'd do more querying. Mostly, I go after people I know, editors I know, other writers to introduce me to editors, etc."

Lauren actually began her writing career as a music reviewer for the *Village Voice* in New York City. "I was a young poet who knew it wouldn't be at all profitable, but wanted to get into print somehow about something I loved. My second talent is music, so I know a little about that. At the time, I had just started going to concerts and saw a David Bowie show that made me think. So I sat down, wrote about it, and I sent an unsolicited manuscript/review of that Bowie concert to "Music Editor, *Village Voice*" when I was 18 — and the (new) editor, Christgau, read it, liked it, wrote back to me, and ultimately hired me to do music reviews for the *Village Voice* many years ago."

For Lauren, the writing process gives "a feeling of time, stopping: there's something so precious and inexplicable about how I feel about writing — and not "being a writer." But yes, once you're hooked, writing's for life. Make friends with editors, be sure to praise all writing you like, and please, please, please make a habit of rewriting and editing so that your words sound effortless and flow like the most wonderful poetry — even if it's NOT poetry!"

Lauren suggests aspiring writers "just get writing about what you're really into and send that copy out to places where other people are writing about similar things and you'll probably get interest."

"Give up. Now. It's not too late to have a "normal" life where you aren't always thinking about the next story, some characters you're developing, a twist on a lyric to a song, a sweet haiku that just came, impromptu…. All right, if the person is dead set on "being a writer," that's nice, but if they're set on really WRITING, I'd say, just GET TO WORK! Start writing every day, every free moment…. You can BE a writer, or you can WRITE. When both happens, that's a career whether you're well paid or constantly struggling. P.S. — Journalism is some of the best practice and experience you can ever have as a writer, so try to pursue it in some way, shape, or form."

Discover What Type of Stories You Like to Write

Being passionate about what you do will automatically lead to success. Your passion and enthusiasm will shine through your work. Writing helps us understand the world and our place in it. But, how do you know what you like to write?

Do you like writing about a hobby? Are you a parent who enjoys writing about the trials of parenthood? Are you burnt out on your current field but have a passion for all things food related? What do you like to read? What types of magazines do you gravitate toward? Are you a news junkie? Who do you follow on Twitter? What topics do you search the Web for?

What Story Ideas Are Marketable

Some well-read, marketable story ideas include:

- **Unusual Events:** Any event that is odd or unusual always makes a good story. People are fascinated with the bizarre, curious, other worldly, and totally out there. The fact that it is out of the ordinary will generate interest in it.

- **Human Interest:** Stories about the human condition are always marketable. People enjoy making human emotional connections to others. For example, the potter who keeps teaching pottery despite losing his arm due to an infection or the child who raises money for a parent going through a terrible disease.

- **Instructional:** How-to stories are always marketable to the right publication. Have a specific hobby or trade that you are an expert in? Use that knowledge to create some pieces to sell to specific audiences.

How Do You Come up with a Story Idea?

There are numerous ways to come up with story ideas. Here are some techniques that might work for you:

- Read, read, read: Read everything you can get your hands on. You never know what will spark a story idea. Books, magazines, newspapers, and blogs can provide you with inspiration for your own ideas.

- Listen to others: What are other people talking about in the office, at the bus stop, at the soccer game?

- Tap into your own experiences: Write about what you know, research the rest.

- Keep a journal: Writing on a daily basis about your observations of the world will help you come up with ideas about topics to write about.

CASE STUDY: WRITING OUT OF A CAREER

Aimée Alley
Energetic Intelligence
Speaker/Teacher/Author/Coach
Littleton, CO
www.sacred-self.net
Aimee@AimeeAlley.com

"It is like birthing a baby. You love your baby and want to protect it. Eventually the baby grows up and must go out into the world."

Aimée has been writing for eight years, four of those as a professional writer. She has a bachelor's degree and has written college papers, keeps a blog and writes in a personal journal.

"Most of my writing has been for workshops or retreats. I also would write up a program for clients as their soul/life coach and did my own private journaling along the way."

Over time, she says, people, participants, and clients would be "asking for a book about the work or suggest that I write a book."

So, Aimée did just that and published a book titled *Heart & Soul — 10 Keys to your Sacred Self*.

"I found the process to be very frightening and exhilarating," she said. "My topics and work are very personal to me as well as those I have worked with. It is like birthing a baby. You love your baby and want to protect it. Eventually the baby grows up and must go out into the world. A very intimidating process when writing isn't my first instinct, it's speaking."

Getting into "the zone" is Aimée's favorite aspect of writing.

"I have been an athlete all my life, and it took me awhile to find the zone in writing.... and there is one. When you get into it and the writing is flowing, I find I just can't stop. Plus, I have learned never to edit along the way.... just write and let it flow.... that is the zone for me!"

When Aimée is in a project, writing becomes a daily exercise that starts early in the morning for four to five hours. When she is not working on a specific project, writing has been seasonal work, around her kids' schedule, during summer vacation.

"I have even tried just taking four days off and going to a cabin to write. That worked to get things started and organized. I thought I might get most of the writing done, because I had a coach that used to write that way and it worked for her... not so much for me. My writing is nonfiction, mostly experiential, meditative, with some research. My workshops, retreats and clients have been my resource for what I write about."

Aimée loves to journal and believes it is a powerful tool for anyone at anytime. "It is a perfect place to document one's life. Journaling enables me to observe my work and make additions or subtractions to what I do. It gives me a great insight into my life and my work."

When it comes to navigating the social media world, Aimée says that "blogging is something I look forward to working with more as I move into my next book.

"I love the exchange of thoughts and discussion with other people that are specific to the topics presented. I have blogged in the past, but I have found that you need to stay consistent to make it work both ways. With publishing a book and getting out into the public as well as maintain my other responsibilities, I have found it hard to make a routine of it. There are so many avenues for a writer to get their work noticed now, and it can be a difficult road to navigate... Facebook, Likened, Pinterest®, Stumble Upon®, blogs, on line magazines etc.... and I am sure there will be more in the near future. Finding the experts and just discussing this with other writers has been a great way to help navigate these opportunities along the way."

Writing about what you know is easy and saves you work. Here are some places to start when trying to figure out what you might enjoy writing about that you have direct knowledge of:

- Dig into your personal life: home, family, personal history, your religion, life experience, and cultural backgrounds are all subjects that you know first-hand about and can authentically create stories from.

- Look at your hobbies and interests: Do you play tennis on weekends? Are you a weekend road warrior? Do you have a knack for genealogy? Do you garden? Raise spiders?

- Your work experience: Do you have a background in business? Have you ever flipped burgers or worked retail? Can you think of any work-related experiences you have had that others might enjoy reading about?

- Schooling: Where did you go to school? What types of classes did you take? What did you major in? Did you live off-campus or on? What activities did you take part in?

- Your personal observations: How do you look at the world around you? What do you think of people who behave in a certain way? Are you a parent? What experiences can you draw on from that?

A sample brainstorming session might look like this:

Broad topic: Pets

Narrow it down: Exotic pets

More detailed: Spiders

Story ideas: How to raise spiders.

How to mate spiders.

How to sell spiders.

How to feed and care for spiders.

What to do if your spiders get loose in the house.

You can also try to develop story topic ideas by:

- Brainstorming on a topic

- Looking at magazines and books; one topic may spark a different type of article or story from your perspective.

- Research a particular topic on the Internet to see what other people are writing or not writing about it.

Sometimes the best thing to do is to stop trying to figure out what to write and sit down and start writing.

Writing prompts: Using writing prompts is a fun way to write. It starts you with an idea, but you can write out the story in your own way.

Finding a Market for Your Ideas (newspaper, magazine, online source)

Knowing where to sell what you write is as important as knowing how to write. While you are learning about the various markets to which you can present your idea or topic, think of these five questions when looking to query a publication:

1. Audience: Does my article fit the audience in this market? Does the audience fit my topic?

2. Market: Does my idea or topic work best in one particular market over another? Can I cross over markets?

3. Fit: Does the market or publication publish my type of idea or topic?

4. Acceptance: Does the market accept freelance work, beginners, or established writers?

5. Payment: Does the market or publication pay? How well? If they do not pay, what do they offer the writer for compensation?

You have plenty of markets to explore that present solid opportunities for publishing your work. The goal is to identify a few of the most popular markets in the industry, with the understanding that you, as a professional writer, will take the liberty to do additional research and uncover more viable markets. Consumer and literary magazines, trade journals, newspapers, and online sources are some of the most common markets to sell your work to.

Consumer magazines

When authors talk about sending query letters to a publication, the most common type that comes to mind is the consumer magazine article. Most writers try to break into this market. Some resources for uncovering available magazines include:

- **www.writersmarket.com:** This website is considered the primary industry resource for finding available magazines to query and writer's guidelines for each publication. You can purchase the annual print version of the publication or subscribe online to a monthly, one-year, or two-year membership.

- **www.writersweekly.com:** This is an online, freelance writing e-zine dedicated to bringing industry news and market opportunities to freelance writers.

- **www.writersdigest.com:** Since 1920, this industry magazine has been devoted to helping writers develop their craft and hone their publishing skills.

- **www.worldwidefreelance.com/writing-markets:** This website was established in 1999 with the goal of publishing a database of freelance markets around the world.

Literary magazines

Start your research online at the Literary Magazines section of **www.pw.org/literary_magazines**. This online source has a comprehensive, searchable database that lists more than 500 literary magazines and journals, along with respective submission guidelines and contact information.

Other notable resources to for finding literary markets include:

- **www.publishersweekly.com:** This trade magazine is published weekly and is the primary resource for booksellers, librarians, and publishers. The magazine reviews on average 5,000 books annually, with the exception of reference books.

- **www.newpages.com/literary-magazines:** NewPages is an online resource that provides news, information, and guides to independent bookstores, literary magazines, independent publishers, alternative periodicals, and other writing outlets.

- **www.everywritersresource.com/literarymagazines:** This website is about writers and their passion for publishing and helping others who are dedicated to the same passion.

- **www.kirkusreviews.com:** This is a biweekly pre-publication newsletter for booksellers, agents, librarians, and publishers that reviews 80 to 100 books per issue. The newsletter reviews nonfiction and fiction works with the exception of poetry, mass-market paperbacks, and children's picture books.

Trade journals

Trade journals are publications that focus on a particular "trade" or industry. The pay for getting publishing in a trade journal varies widely. If you have a particular expertise or specialization, you can stand out in this market because it is a great outlet to establish yourself as an expert in a specific line of business. Just as there are consumer magazines for just about every topic you can think of, there are trade journals for just about every business.

Typical resources for locating trade journals include:

- **www.oxbridge.com:** This directory provides detailed contact information, editorial descriptions, target audiences, and other helpful information for more than 14,000 U.S. and Canadian consumer, business, and association newsletters.

- **http://us.cision.com:** This comprehensive directory contains in-depth information about all daily and community newspapers published in the U.S. and Canada, as well as 21,700 trade and consumer magazines, newsletters, and journals.

- **www.gale.cengage.com:** This directory details more than 162,000 nonprofit member organizations worldwide and provides contact information and descriptions of professional societies, trade associations, fan clubs, and organizations.

These publications are best referenced at your local library. Because the publishers of these directories produce these publications annually, it might not be cost-effective to purchase them outright. They can cost anywhere from $175 to $650.

The general writing protocol for trade magazines is to write more with a tone of facts and information rather than creativity. People who subscribe to trade journals are looking for relevant, timely information that will help them learn a new skill or provide professional development opportunities. Not often the first market to come to a writer's mind, trade journals can be a lucrative industry. They offer a variety of other benefits, including a steady source of income if you are an expert in the field, an opportunity to stay current on a particular field of interest as you will need to be researching continually to keep up with changes in the industry, and the opportunity to build a solid base of clients who will afford you the opportunity to work on other projects.

In most cases, writers who submit articles to trade journals might not be completely familiar with the industry, especially if they are just getting started in their writing career. Therefore, it is a good idea for writers who want to pursue the trade journal market to work with a mentor. This mentor should be a member of the industry who can advise on the issues and provide the writer with direction. Email makes it easier to approach an industry mentor.

Start your search by looking at biographies at the end of articles related to your topic. You also can check with professional associations and networks to find a mentor. Use a search engine or a phone book to hunt down trade organizations or a local chapter. For example, if you want to write about fishing but are not a fisher, locate a local sportsman club and get to know its members. People often are willing to share their knowledge with you if you show interest. Once you have found a potential mentor, craft a professional email, and send it off asking him or her if he or she might consider being your mentor or if he or she can refer someone who might be interested in being a mentor. Or find out if their meetings are open to the public and head to the meeting to research your topic.

A sample email might look like this:

```
Mr. Engstrom:

I am a writer who is interested in writing
about fishing for trout. I was wondering if you
might be able to help me with my research so
that I can really understand the topic I wish
to write about.

Does your sportsman club have meetings or get-
togethers that are open to the public, where I
might be able to talk to some of your members
about their tips on trout fishing?

Thank you for you time. I can be reached by
email at the above address or by phone at
(888) 222-4444.

Best regards,

Jane Writer
```

Newspapers

The most important lesson you will need to learn when trying to corner the newspaper market is technique: Prepare yourself to work as efficiently as possible against tight deadlines. This type of scenario oftentimes produces some of the best writers. Very few environments can force a writer to organize, prioritize, and deliver more than a newspaper. The top industry resources for the newspaper market include:

- **www.editorandpublisher.com:** This journal has roots that date back to 1884. It is America's oldest journal covering all aspects of the newspaper industry from business and newsroom to syndicates and circulation.

- **www.asne.org:** Founded in 1922, this nonprofit professional organization focuses on leadership development, innovation, policies, and journalism topics.

- **www.altweeklies.com:** AAN was founded in Seattle, Washington, in 1978 and is a conglomerate of 130 alt-weekly news organizations covering every major metropolitan area of North America.

Online publications

Online publications are basically magazines, journals, or news-letters published on the Internet. The pay for this market varies greatly, but the opportunities are endless, and online publications seem to be more open to freelance writers. When you are first starting out, however, be prepared to take a job on the low end of the payment spectrum until you gain some more experience. It is becoming more acceptable and almost a necessity to have online magazine publishing as part of your clips lineup.

Many novice writers make the mistake of having a more relaxed demeanor when it comes to online publications. Online writing might not appear to have as many formal guidelines due to the large amount of writing on the Web done in blog form by just anybody, but if you are pursuing writing as a professional, you should approach online writing that way as well. Just because a factual error or typo can be changed in a second does not mean it will not be seen by hundreds if not thousands of people before your publication can make the change, and you do not want even a trace of unprofessionalism to enter your writing at any time. If you think your readers will not notice, think again. The blessing and curse of the Internet is that anyone can search any topic at any time. Your readers *will* judge you and your future bylines if they come across any mistakes.

Regardless of the medium, writers should approach a publication with the same enthusiasm and professionalism. Editors are editors, both online and off. Just as with any of the other markets,

querying might vary greatly depending on the requirements of the publication you approach. Some submission guidelines are more stringent than others.

Writing for an online publication is a worthwhile endeavor if you do your homework before querying the publication. The approach to an online publication is the same as a traditional publication. Start with some of these valuable resources to learn more about getting your work published in online publications:

- **www.writersonlineworkshops.com:** *Writer's Digest*® provides an online, state-of-the-art learning environment dedicated to writing instruction. The Web-based university combines world-class writing courses with on-demand training.

- **www.writermag.com:** This monthly industry magazine is considered an essential resource for writers. It provides advice and inspiration for today's writer through feature articles, literary markets, practical solutions, tips from famous authors, and profiles of selected literary magazines.

If you are just starting out and looking for a flexible market, online publishing might be a reliable source. Focus your attention on smaller, local publications (after ensuring they are reputable) and work your way up to the more well-known publications. Build your clip file and your earning potential by writing for a variety of markets and publications.

Research, research, research

I cannot stress enough how important it is to do your research. Numerous options are out there for writing jobs, and the only way to discover which best suits you, is by research. Set aside blocks of time to research everything you can. Head to the library or the bookstore and look through all the different types of magazines on the market. Hit the Web. Research the salability of different topics. Discover what types of writing opportunities are out there.

Make lists of your favorite topics and research the different types of publications that might consider an article with those topics in mind. Research various publications guidelines. Find out the specifics on different publications and their requirements.

Check out what is trending on the Internet by going to sites like **www.google.com** and **www.yahoo.com**. Simply type in the keywords "trending" and you will be able to discover what hot topics people are searching for on the Internet. These trending topics might lead to a great story idea for you to write about.

You are on a journey of discovery; this is your chance to find out everything you can on your road to being a successful writer.

Chapter 4

SETTING UP SHOP

"I can only write when I am inspired, and I see to it that I am inspired at nine o'clock every morning."

— Peter de Vries, editor and novelist

If you worked in an office, you typically would be assigned a desk and a chair at which to work. If you worked at a florist, you would most likely have a space on which to cut flowers and create arrangements. Why should writing be any different? Luckily, as writers, we have the benefit of being able to work from anywhere. All we need is a pen and paper or a laptop, and we are ready to go.

It is easy, however, to get sucked into buying all the tools of the trade. But, do you really need that brand new, shiny flat-screened gadget that promises to make your life easier? Or that fabulous desk chair that is programmable to the contours of your body? It might make things easier, but you probably do not need all that to get started.

What you do need, however, is a dedicated work space.

Creating a Dedicated Work Space

Being able to work from anywhere is one of the best perks of being a freelance writer. That being said, having a dedicated work space is just as important for those times you really need to concentrate on a project. It also gives you a landing pad to file paperwork, make important phone calls, and mentally be able to "check-in" to your workday. A dedicated work space that is your own also solidifies that writing, as passionate as you are about it, is also a serious job, not to be taken lightly.

I have been known to work in my car, at a picnic table on the patio, sitting up in bed, at the dining room table, tucked into the corner of the couch, and at my kitchen island. This is mostly out of necessity when I need to keep an eye on the kids, watch the pot so it does not boil over on the stove, wait for a delivery, or even help with homework in-between news stories.

I also, however, have a dedicated workspace for when I need absolute quiet and have to concentrate on meeting a deadline. One day, I hope to have an entire room dedicated to my writing that I can fill with my favorite books, inspirational paintings, a comfortable chair for reading, and an amazing antique French writing desk. Even better, it would be located in the countryside of a small French village. What do we have if not our dreams?

In the meantime, however, I have a plain black desk tucked into an alcove in our bedroom that sits underneath a sunny window from which I can hear the sounds of our wooded property. On my desk sits two beaded lamps, a container with an assortment of pens and markers, some pretty writing stationary, research books and a host of other miscellaneous items like file folders and an empty teacup from working late the night before. It is not "perfect," but it is perfect for what a dedicated space needs to be — it has good lighting, supplies, a place to file paperwork, and a quiet space to get work done.

Here are some things to consider when finding a dedicated writing space in your house:

- Location, location, location is key.
- Do you like noise, soothing sounds, or silence when you write?

- Do you need to be able to set up a desktop computer, or will you be working on a laptop?
- Do you like natural lighting when you work, or do you prefer to shut out the outside world?
- Do you need space for research materials, or will most of your research be done online?
- Do you need access to a phone line, or will you conduct your business on a cell phone?
- Do you need space for a file drawer?
- Will you need an outlet to plug in a phone, laptop, or light?
- Do you need to be able to keep an eye on the kids or pets while you work?

Possible locations in your house for a dedicated writing space might include:

- An under-used closet. Take the doors off and push a small desk into the space to create an instant writing nook. Or build a desk with a piece of plywood and two filing cabinets as the base to fit the exact dimension of the closet.

- Do you really need that guest bedroom that sits empty 90 percent of the time? Put a desk in there to create a dedicated writing space while still allowing you a guest bedroom during the times you do have out-of-town visitors.

- Add a sofa table behind the couch that can do double-duty as a desk. Let your family know that this is your space and is off limits to their "stuff."

- Tuck a desk in the corner of the dining room behind a screen room divider.

- Commandeer a corner of your bedroom.

- Make room in the basement, garage, or attic. With the right lighting and a little bit of creativity, you can create a sanctuary space perfect for writing in an unused corner.

CASE STUDY: DEDICATING WRITING SPACE AS A SANCTUARY

Susan Marek
susan@susanmarek.com
www.susanmarek.com

"It is important for me to have a space that is solely my own because it becomes a sanctuary for me while writing." Susan Marek

Susan Marek has been writing for enjoyment her entire life and has been writing professionally for about three years. In addition to college papers, magazine and newspaper articles, Web page content, business materials, and online articles, Susan also has written newsletters and fliers and writes a personal blog. She also keeps a journal on a regular basis.

Susan's writing has always been a side project, but it is quickly becoming her day job. She wrote stories in grade school and was published for the first time in the local paper when she was in sixth grade. Susan also has been a freelance writer; she wrote articles on local businesses and a meditation article for an online newsletter. She recently published a children's book on the chakras that was nominated as a finalist in About.com's annual Readers' Choice Award competition. She also currently is working on a handful of other book projects as she pursues writing as a full-time endeavor. Her website and blog state that Susan helps "empower people to live an authentic, divine life, filled with light and integrity" through her writing, workshops, and mentoring.

When it comes to writing on a regular basis, Susan needs to schedule her writing to fit it into her day, but has not been able to do it yet. Right now, she says, she writes when she can and when she is most inspired. "I love creating pictures with words and trying to share my imagination through writing," Susan said. It is something she has wanted to do since she was young.

To help motivate herself, Susan recently revamped her workspace. "I found a place in my home that has a gorgeous view of trees and other landscape. I put a bird feeder and birdbath outside the window so I would have beautiful visitors throughout the day. Because my work-space was cluttered and energetically chaotic, I invested in a new set of desk furniture." The space, she says, enables her to have a place for her research material that is close at hand, as well as a hiding place for those items that could be a distraction from writing.

"It is important for me to have a space that is solely my own because it becomes a sanctuary for me while writing," she said.

She even added some personal things to her writing space. "I have a tapestry that I bought on a recent trip to France that is a reminder of why I write. I am surrounded by my favorite books that constantly inspire me. I even have a few fortunes from some fortune cookies that sit on my desk above my keyboard."

Susan suggests you find some items to make your space your own. It can be a favorite pen or a special rock from a family vacation that makes your space *yours*, she says. Whatever it is, it is important that you add it to your special, sacred writing space for inspiration.

"When I first decided to carve out a space in my home for this, I had a difficult time finding a place. It wasn't that I didn't have the room. It was more about committing to myself that this space was for writing and that I deserved it. I am a writer, an author, and I had to embrace that title to move past the block that maybe I had nothing to say, therefore I didn't need a place to write. After that, creating the space was fun, and now I am more inspired than ever!"

Tips for making the space your own include:

- Add a favorite photo to your workspace.
- Hang an inspirational picture above your writing space.
- Display your pens in a favorite mug.
- Create a stack of your favorite books.
- Add a flowering plant or nice smelling herb in a pretty pot.
- Place little reminders like shells, stones, or figurines of your favorite vacations, etc. on your desk.

Finding a space of your own will help you commit to your passion of becoming a successful writer. It will validate the process and allow you to embrace that you are, in fact, a writer. Creating a dedicated writing space also will signal to your family that when you are in that space, you are "working." Do not forget to add personal touches to make it your own — a favorite pen, an inspirational quote, a photograph of your favorite place, etc. As a writer, you need a healthy combination of functionality and inspiration.

What Tools You *Really* Need

Luckily, there is very little you actually need to get started as a writer. Here are the basics:

- Private workspace (or at least a corner on a table to get started):

As discussed in the previous section, a private workspace is paramount when trying to get work done, talk to a client, or just recognize that you are in "work mode"

- Good lighting for your workspace

- A flat space to spread out notes, books, and other "tools"

- A place to file notes, articles, correspondences, invoices, etc.

- A shelf to hold your most precious reference books (like this one)

- Computer: As a freelance writer, you will need a computer to correspond via email with clients, to do research, and even to write on. If you are serious about freelancing, a computer of your very own is an essential item. Ideally, you will have your own computer and not one that is a "shared family computer." This item, if nothing else, should be your first business expense.

- A good chair with proper support, as you will be spending lots of time sitting in it.

- A good Internet connection

- A phone

- An email account dedicated to your writing career (more on that later)

Setting Aside Time

Writers write. Like any other ambition, writing requires a dedication to the craft. Major league baseball players get to where they are by practicing, practicing, and practicing their sport. Likewise, to be a successful writer, one needs to practice the art of writing. Some days, the words will flow easily. Others, it will seem like trying to squeeze blood from a stone.

Regardless, successful writers make time to write each day. How can you do this in between the full-time job, dropping the kids off at soccer practice, making dinner, doing laundry, etc.? If becoming a freelance writer is important to you, finding time to write is a necessity.

It can seem like a large obstacle sometimes to try to fit writing in among all the other priorities you face, but do not lose heart. Here are a few helpful hints you can follow to developing a writing schedule:

- Keep track of your time. For a week, write down all the activities you performed in a given day. Document how much time you spent on each activity. Do not leave anything out, even if it was not related to writing. Your list should include time spent shopping, surfing the Internet, going to the gym, sleeping, taking classes, etc. At the end of the week, you will have a pretty good idea of where your time is being spent.

- Cut out what you do not need. If you need to schedule writing time, you now should be able to identify which activities can be removed. If you are having trouble cutting out what you do not need, then start prioritizing the activities into "A," "B," and "C" categories with "A" being the highest priority. Once you have prioritized them, try to temporarily remove all or most of the "C" activities (or at least cut back on them significantly), recalculate your hours, and see how much time you have recovered for writing. If you have cut out everything you can and still need some more time, try combining tasks.

- Combine tasks if you can. Some activities will be impossible or very difficult to cut from your schedule; so look at the activities that remain and see if there is anything left on your list that could be combined and done simultaneously. In other words, see if there are two or more things you can multitask on to save yourself more time for writing. For example, you could read the newspaper and work out at the same time.

- Take advantage of extra time. A few minutes here, a few minutes there can add up to some extra time you can allocate to writing your queries. A common problem with finding extra time is that it might not be used productively. If your extra time is only ten minutes, it is probably not a good idea to work on a 1,000-word article. However, in those ten minutes, you probably can research another market, send off an email to request a sample copy of a publication, or jot down a brief outline for a query topic. If you have an extra hour or two of time, then you can dedicate that time to flushing out your query letter. Every minute counts, so do not wait to get a large block of time to sit down and write. Use the time you have found, schedule writing time on your calendar, and be sure to start with small, manageable activities.

- The closer you get to publication, the more your writing work increases. A writing schedule is imperative to be successful. If you have mastered your writing schedule and figured out how to make it work with your other responsibilities, you are well on your way to developing a winning edge.

CASE STUDY: FINDING TIME TO WRITE

Beth Tiger
Owner
A Life Well Lived, LLC
alifewelllivedllc@gmail.com
www.alifewelllived.com
www.bethtiger.com

"I am a mom and business owner, so finding time to write sometimes means 12 at night when everyone else is sleeping." Beth Tiger

A busy business owner, wife, and mother, Beth Tiger has been writing professionally for 18 years, recreationally for 24, and considers herself "just getting started" as a writer. She is a certified life coach and has experience writing magazine and newspaper articles as well as Web page content, business materials, newspapers, and books. She also has kept a journal since her teen years.

Beth has been published in several new age and healthy lifestyle publications since the 1990s. She has written on coaching topics, as well as metaphysical topics, and used to write a paid aromatherapy column for Inner Realm newspaper. She was asked to write the aromatherapy column because she "was one of the only 'certified' and properly trained aromatherapists in the tristate area back in the early 90s."

Beth also has written numerous newsletters. "When I opened my first metaphysical shop, I created a newsletter," she says. Currently, she writes a monthly and bimonthly newsletter for her wellness center. She also creates workshop formats and her first book is set to be published by June of 2012. She considers writing a part of her full time job as a business owner.

Between all of her commitments, Beth has to fit writing into her schedule whenever she can.

"I work on my newsletter at my office, and if I am asked to provide an article, I will fit it in where I can."

When she wrote her book, Beth found that she had to "dedicate serious time to the process without distraction. It took me several years to understand why the book was not coming together. I lost my train of thought and found that writing from home and stopping and starting was the biggest issue (I could always find something to distract me from the writing like a load of wash, dishes in the sink, etc.)."

As a result, Beth decided to go to her country house alone and spent several days up there with no access to the Internet. "This was the solution for me," she said. "The words poured out, and I was able to wrap up the book in a matter of days. Heck, I had nothing else to do but walk (which helped me a lot when I was blocked), eat, sleep, and write."

Beth started on her writing journey to "get the messages that I felt weren't out in the public out there." Her favorite aspect of writing is seeing the completed project, something that was in her mind "becoming manifest on paper." She says that getting support from other writers is paramount to being a successful writer. Writers need to "*Write*. Be open to constructive advice, then apply it."

Pros of Organization, Dangers of Procrastination

So many things can distract a writer in the course of their "workday." There are the basic household items like laundry, cleaning, and meal preparation. Then there is refereeing the kids' fights, taking the dog for a walk, cleaning out the refrigerator.... you get my drift. Not to mention that does not even include distractors like television and searching the Internet. Oftentimes, we whine that there just is not "enough hours in the day" to get everything done. How are you possibly going to add writing into your already packed day?

Personally, I happen to be an excellent procrastinator. I can find just about anything to distract me from what I "should" be doing. To help combat my tendency to procrastinate, I need to set deadlines for myself and schedule household chores so they do not interfere with my writing time. Being extremely organized also is helpful to getting everything done. Being organized saves time, which actually gives me more time to do the things I do when I procrastinate.

Being efficient with your writing will keep you organized. As a newbie, you might spend more time laboring over every word and every sentence because you want things to be just right. As you become more skilled with querying and writing assignments, you will learn what to focus on first and what to tweak and perfect later. Laboring only adds to procrastination, and procrastination is not a writer's friend.

Some writers spend time waiting for the right inspiration, the right block of time, and the right environment. If you wait for all the elements to be perfectly in line, you will be wasting valuable time. An effective way to increase your writing time and maximize your productivity is to develop and adhere to a writing routine. This writing routine might look something like:

- **Inspiration and idea time:** This is time you allocate for thinking, brainstorming, and gathering snippets of inspiration. This time might require you to be away from the TV, the computer, and other people. You might have heard of stories from people who get their best ideas while they are in the shower or on a walk. The goal of the inspiration and idea time is to allow for purely brain-based freethinking.

- **Researching time:** Once you have obtained inspiration and gathered new ideas, additional research might be needed to further develop an idea. Before hopping on the Internet or taking a trip to the library, write out your plan of attack. Develop a checklist or bullet points of the questions you need to answer or the problems you need to solve. Jot down relevant keywords or word strings that will help to refine your search. Once you find the information you need, clip, extract, or copy and paste it to a document for future reference. Do not forget to cite the source.

- **Planning time:** Your planning time involves writing your outline or creating a mind map of how you intend to approach your assignment. You can fill in the details of this rough outline later, but at least, you will have a basis from which to start developing content.

- **Content development time:** With your research facts and outline handy, it is time to just start writing. The objective of the content development time is to just write; do not worry about editing or filling in the facts. If there is a word or statistic you do not have at this time, just highlight it and keep going. The idea during this time is to keep the flow going. Write as long as you can, and stop when you get tired. Writing when you are tired drains your creative juices and your ability to write fast.

- **Editing time:** Start by reading aloud what you have developed. It might seem uncomfortable for you at first, but reading aloud helps you quickly identify errors or parts that need to be restructured. After you have identified those sections that have errors or need rewriting, go back to the areas you highlighted and begin filling in the information or facts. Once you have everything filled in and fixed, do another edit. If time permits, see if you can have another person edit it before you submit.

- **Downtime:** Before starting this sequence all over again, give yourself a break. Take some time to be away from the grind, or you will burn out. Use your down time to focus on you and your personal goals. Maybe go to the gym, spend time with your family, go out with friends, or do some volunteer work. The purpose of the down time is to refuel and prepare to start your writing routine again.

Practicing this writing routine will help you write faster, better, and more easily in the future. It might be a slow start at first because you are not used to it. Every writer has his or her own system, but having a guideline to start from can help you transition into your own personal tool. The trick or secret behind writing faster is about being organized and prepared. Creating a sense of structure to your writing and your writing schedule allows ideas to flow easily and quickly. It also helps you avoid procrastinating on work-related tasks.

Next to scheduling time for writing, tracking submissions is another critical activity that will require your attention. Believe it or not, submissions do get lost in the mail and editors inadvertently can delete or misplace your electronic query. So, do not rely on editors, agents, and publishers to help you manage and keep track of your markets, submissions, and contacts. This responsibility is solely up to you, and a variety of tools are available to help you success-

fully keep track of your submissions. The most commonly used methods for tracking queries submissions are: computer spreadsheets, desktop submission tracking software, and online submission trackers.

Computer spreadsheets are one of the simplest tracking tools available because, nowadays, most everyone has a spreadsheet program on their computers. The most common program is Microsoft® Excel®. Another increasingly popular spreadsheet is Google Docs, which offers an online spreadsheet in the lineup. The most important aspect of creating a tracking submission spreadsheet is to design it with the correct and most useful headers. The headings listed below are generic. You might find that you need more fields that are tailored to your genre or personal tracking preferences.

Spreadsheets are the simplest and most cost-effective way to track your query submissions. Once you have established the fields, you quickly can fill in the information relevant to each query. As you add more queries, the spreadsheet allows you to sort your information on any of the fields.

Using the spreadsheet approach offers you basic functionality, which can be a good way to track your submissions, as you are first starting out.

Software companies that specialize in products for writers, publishers, and agents often develop desktop submission tracking software. You can purchase this software on a CD or download it from the company's website. As mentioned in the previous section, there might come a time when you outgrow your spreadsheet and need to move to something more robust to manage the size of your growing submissions.

Online submission trackers are usually Web-based communities where the user creates an account (free or at a monthly subscription rate. The primary benefit of online submission trackers is that you can access your information while you are away from your home or office computer. These online tracking applications offer services that allow you to track the markets you approach, the status of the queries you have submitted, estimated response times, publication guidelines, query titles, money earned from each sale, editors' comments, and pay rates.

You also can use these tools to organize your other "responsibilities" outside of your writing work. Spreadsheets are a great way to schedule your household chores, for example. Or, you can take advantage of a host of free apps for your mobile device to help you get organized. Learning to multitask also will help you feel less frazzled. For example, throw in a load of laundry or run the dishwasher just before you sit down to write for an hour. After the hour is up, take a break from writing to fold the laundry or put away the dishes.

Learning to organize your daily tasks and avoiding procrastination are paramount to becoming a successful writer. That being said, keep in mind that it is a process and every day will not fall into a perfect schedule of organized bliss. The car will break down, the kids' schedules will change, your spouse will be homesick and require your attention, and you may have to shift your priorities.

Your Writing Career Goals

Setting goals is a necessary part of becoming a successful freelance writer. If you do not know where you want to go, how will you know when you get there? Because a freelance writer does not have a typical "boss," there is no one to let you know what to do, how to do it, and when to get it done. One way to move beyond not having anyone to answer to is to set goals for yourself. In order to be effective, your writing goals should be attainable, meaningful, and measurable.

For a goal to be measurable, for example, it must be something that is quantifiable. To have a goal of becoming a "good writer" is an excellent goal, but how can you measure that? One can always become a "better" writer. A measurable goal would be something more like planning to write a certain number of pagers per work or spend a specific amount of hours writing each day.

Goals also can help you by breaking up your writing career dreams into smaller, more attainable steps. If your goal is to become a best-selling author, but you have never written a paragraph outside of a holiday letter, you might want to consider setting a smaller goal like attending a writing workshop or selling a story idea to an online newspaper. To set attainable goals, you need to be completely honest with yourself and determine what is possible for you given your other responsibilities and what you can commit to writing.

Setting goals for yourself also needs to be meaningful. You may dream of writing that great novel, but you also may need to pay the rent. Consequently, you may feel like you have to give up on that novel in order to do the responsible thing and put food on the table. But, what if there is a compromise? Perhaps, you can spend 80 percent of your working time focused on writing jobs that pay the rent and the other 20 percent of your time delving into your historical fiction novel? In order for your goals to be meaningful to you, you also need to define what "success" as a writer means to you.

Another effective goal-setting tool is to divide your goals into one of two categories: short and long-term goals. A healthy mix of both will put you on the right track and steer you in the direction of becoming a successful freelance writer. Where do you want to be in six months, a year, five years, ten years? Those would be examples of long-term goals whereas how many hours do you want to spend working on writing per day would fall into the short-term category.

Once you set your goals, you will need to hold yourself account-able to them. The best way to do this is to write your goals down and then check in on your progress periodically. You even can have fun with it and reward yourself when you reach certain goals.

Here is a sample of what a goal-tracking chart might look like:

Goal	Time-frame	Completed	Notes
Write 1-2 hours per week	Month of June	YES!	Increase hours goal for next month; that was too easy!
Build as many clips as possible	Next 6 months	YES!	Now have over 10 clips to use as samples for future jobs.

Goal	Time-frame	Completed	Notes
Designate a writing space	By end of the week	YES!	I found a corner to put my desk in the spare room, but would eventually like a dedicated office for my work.
Get published in a magazine	Within 6 months	YES!	*Renaissance Magazine* purchased a short article on making honey wine. Set a new goal of coming up with more ideas to query to Ren Mag.
Send out a minimum of 10 queries per week	For the next month	Fell a little short	I was only able to average 6-8 queries per week. Will try again next month.
Find a part-time job that will allow me to dedicate more time to writing	Within 6 months	Not yet.	Keep looking! Perhaps I should use my current full-time income to set aside some padding money when I do find a part-time job.
Purchase a dedicated work laptop	Within 2 months	Not yet	I found one that is reasonable and just need to save for another few weeks before I can purchase it.

Do not worry about not hitting the goals you have set for yourself. They are intended to be guidelines, not something that locks you in to any one thing. Goals will morph and change over time as you develop as a writer. Be willing to be flexible and go with the flow. Goals are not your dream; they are just a tool to help you attain your dreams.

Chapter 5

HOW TO MARKET YOURSELF

"There are three difficulties in authorship: to write anything worth publishing — to find honest men to publish it — and to get sensible men to read it."

— Charles Caleb Cotton,
writer, collector, and poet

Having the skills to write is only part of being a successful writer. In addition, you will need to know how to market yourself successfully. To do so, you will need a writing portfolio of clips, a good website, and know how to use social media. The first step in marketing yourself is to develop you as a brand.

Regardless of writing goals, you are a brand. That is a reality of being in business, whether for an agent, editor, or publisher or for yourself. Developing a strong personal brand can be a challenging aspect of a writer's career. In an increasingly competitive market, personal branding is imperative, but does not need to be intimidating.

To be successful in the writing industry and to continue developing your career as a professional writer, you will need to develop a reputation that complements your writing skill. Here are some tips for building up your brand:

- **Be unique.** In this type of industry, being a copycat is probably one of the worst offenses against your colleagues. There is nothing wrong with gaining inspiration from others, but work on developing a uniqueness of your own. You will have your own writing style, and your brand needs to convey that same style. Work with a branding expert or read a handful of the personal branding books that are available at your local library or bookstore. Spend some time thinking about what you want to convey about yourself, your work, and your reputation.

- **Consider using a pen name.** One path to follow when developing a personal brand is to write under a pen name. This is particularly common in the fiction genre. Some writers use a name to avoid revealing their true identity. Other writers use a pen name to enhance the brand of their writing style and genre focus.

- **Be consistent.** Consistency is what brings loyalty. If you continue to follow through on your promises and produce what your readers expect, they will come to rely on you. You will create your own personal following, and they will look to you and your writing to meet their needs. One of the primary components of a strong personal brand is your ability to be and remain consistent. That does not mean you have to stagnate. It means you have to remain true to your commitments and continue to stand on the uniqueness you developed from the beginning.

- **Be authentic.** The public can be brutal when critiquing works of art. Just read some of the reviews written about the movies that come out in the theaters. Also read through some of the reviews written about newly released fiction books by some of the nation's best-selling authors. Not all best-selling authors get glowing reviews every time they publish new books. Regardless of the reviews (positive or negative), your goal is to be authentic. Your authenticity is what will keep your readers coming back. Know when to admit your mistakes and faults. Let your readers see a little bit of your humanity so they can connect with you and feel that they know you.

- **Manage your brand.** As the saying goes, "If you do not manage your brand, someone else will." Keep reinventing and managing your personal brand. It should grow with you throughout your career. If you do not manage it, others will take it and run with it. The result might be something that does not represent you well. It will be harder to change your audiences' mind about you once someone else has redefined your brand for you.

Branding yourself, however, does not and should not limit who you are as a writer. For example, I have been able to brand myself as a travel writer, an expert gardening writer, a successful business writer, and a news-style online journalist to name a few incarnations. My next endeavor is as a historic fiction novelist that will draw on my experiences writing for *Renaissance Magazine* and my passion for medieval history. Having a varied writing background also gave me the opportunity to write this book. The secret is being able to tailor yourself through your résumé, your clip samples, and your expertise based on your current place on your writing journey. Traveling and gardening are hobbies of mine that led to a great topic to write on, where I could be authentic with minimal research. I could sell myself as a business writer because I had worked in corporate communications for years and had the résumé to prove it. I could work on news-style journalism pieces because I had a degree in journalism and a passion about the local town I live in.

The secret is using what experiences you have and effectively marketing them to sell yourself as a writer. And, what you do not know, be sure to research, research, research to fill the gaps.

Your Writing Portfolio / Résumé

Like anyone looking for work, a writer needs a good portfolio and résumé. The best way a freelance writer can attract new writing work is by showing off examples of what you have already done as a writer. In the old days, that would mean collecting print pieces that you had a byline on or collaborated on and pulling them together into a binder or work portfolio that you would cart with you to various potential clients.

Today, that means pulling together your clips and showcasing them in an easy-to-access location online, like a website. You also will need electronic copies of your work to send off via email, should a client request them that way. Ideally, you also should have a quick one-page résumé that highlights your writing expertise and is focused on the types of writing jobs you want to get.

A writing portfolio is going to be a work in progress, morphing as you expand your writing horizons and get more and more work. At a certain point, you even may need to create separate portfolios for different genres. An effective way to organize your clips would be to create different folders on your computer. For example, you might create a system that looks like the following:

- Folder name: Travel clips
  - o Subfolder: Domestic
    - Subfolder: Beach vacations
    - Subfolder: Mountain retreats
  - o Subfolder: International
    - Subfolder: Europe
    - Subfolder: Asia

- • Subfolder: Travel packing tips
- • Folder name: Business clips
  - o Subfolder: Newsletters
  - o Subfolder: White papers
    - • Subfolder: Technology
    - • Subfolder: Marketing
  - o Subfolder: Website copy

Organizing your clips will make it easier to find them when you need to send off samples to a potential client. Because people work in a variety of formats, it is important to ensure you follow instructions and format details when sending clips to a client. When in doubt, ask. Most people, however, can read a PDF file. Visit **www.adobe.com** for more information on creating and sending PDF files.

When just starting out as a writer, you will need to be creative in pulling together a clip portfolio since you may not have a lot of work experience writing. The first step is to write your writing résumé. In some cases, you may not even use your writing résumé to send to potential clients, but it will help give you a starting place to help sell yourself as a writer and get you in the mind frame of being a writer.

Writing résumés vary slightly from a traditional résumé in that they highlight your writing skill and not necessarily your prior employment. For example, if you were an administrative assistant, much of your job probably centered on writing business correspondences. Just include one or two bulleted points on your résumé about that. The same goes for all jobs, just pull out the points that are applicable to the craft of writing.

A writing résumé should also include basic résumé items like your name, relevant contact information, and your education. Feel free to include some hobbies or interests if it pertains to topics you hope to write about. If it does not, less is more and drop it.

Some tips for finding clips to include in your writer's portfolio:

- Did you write a letter on behalf of the PTO to a local business?

- Did you help rewrite a letter your boss was sending to a client?

- Were you angry about poor service and wrote a letter to the company asking for your money back?

- Did you create a flier for your neighbor's lost pet?

- Did you write an amazing paper in college on a specific topic?

- Get creative, have a brainstorming session and look at anything in your work and personal life that had you using words to get your point across.

In addition to creating a file and building up your portfolio and résumé of writing clips, you will want to broadcast to the world what you are capable of. That is where a website comes in handy.

Create a Website

Every professional writer should have a professional website. Your website should be a landing pad for readers, editors, and potential employers to discover more about who you are as a writer. But, first, you must determine who that "person" you are trying to sell is. Are you a magazine writer and need a place to show off your clips? Are you trying to sell your novel? Or, are you trying to establish yourself as a business writer, willing to take on any corporate writing job? To determine what focus your website should have, make a list of your goals as a writer and keep those goals in mind as you work through your website design.

Must haves on your website include:

1. A short bio describing your experiences and expertise

2. Quality writing samples where potential clients can see what they would be getting from you as a writer

3. Contact information so that people can get in touch with you

4. Social media connections so people can find you on places like Facebook, Twitter, etc. Do not link to your personal social media places. Instead, you will need to set up business accounts to keep it professional.

A good website should avoid the following:

1. Too much personal information. Your goal is to advance your writing, not talk about your kids (you can always do that on your personal Facebook page). This does not mean you cannot put anything personal on your writer's Web page, you should just ensure it is relevant to your work first.

2. Unpublished writings. Editors will not come to your website looking for the next great story. Posting unpublished, "available" work will give off the message that you cannot get it published so you stuck it on your Web page.

3. A cluttered, messy layout. Keep it simple and professional looking for results.

The best way to get ideas for websites is by researching online. What websites are you drawn to? What kind of websites do other writers have out there? Are they easy to navigate? Can you find all relevant information when you need it? Take a cue from the industry and determine what does and does not work. Head to the library and peruse books on how to set up a successful website. Or search online for information on how to get started. Many free resources are out there. You even may find a local extension course on creating a business website. Take it. (The cost is a business expense, by the way).

Using Social Media

We need to be more than just good writers to get recognized in the current writing climate. We need to develop social media savvy. In today's age, social media is being used as a platform to make a name for yourself and get information about what you are doing out to the world. Each day, it seems as if a new outlet hits the airwaves like Facebook, Twitter, Foursquare®, Pinterest, Tumbler, LinkedIn®, Klout®, etc. How do you know which ones to use and which ones not to use?

The benefit of using what social media has to offer outweighs the negatives of having to keep up. Today, information is shared instantaneously via the Web and unless you are part of that information flow, you will get left behind. Consider social media as a tool that helps promote your brand and who you are.

Social media can help a writer:

1. Connect: It gives an opportunity for colleagues, current clients, potential clients, customers, editors, agents, etc., to come together and share interests, find resources, and ask questions.

2. Monitor your brand online: Social media helps you find out what others are saying about your story, your book, and whether they like it or you need to work on your skill.

3. Research: Social media helps you to understand your clients, your readers, your market, and to search for what is trending and might work for future writing projects.

4. Provide Inspiration and encouragement on your writing journey: It lets you inspire and reach more people than just through your written copy.

5. Helps you provide information on your current projects and upcoming needs.

Some tips when using social media include:

- Find your voice and be consistent.
- Assert your point of view and be heard.
- Think before you push anything out via social media.

Blogging

An increasing number of people are writing blogs and reading blogs. A blog is a Web log, or online journal. It can take the form of a personal journal, a business diary, or even an informational catchall. So, why should you blog?

Here's why:

- Blogs are a great marketing tool.

- They can be updated at any time from anywhere and have a lasting presence on the Internet.

- Blogs facilitate conversation, communication, and share knowledge.

- Blogs will help build your portfolio of writing clips.

- Blogs will give you a presence online.

CASE STUDY: SUCCESSFUL BOOK REVIEWER AND BLOGGER

Tim Larison
tmlarison@gmail.com
www.calmwithin.com
www.timlarison.com
www.familytravelgurus.com^{SM}

"If you are just starting out as a published author, like I am, I think blogging is a good way to start." Tim Larison

Tim Larison has been writing for the fun of it for about 32 years and as a professional writer for the last year or so. He has written college papers, website content, business materials, online articles, and newsletters/fliers, and he is a current book reviewer and blogger. Larison's first experience in getting his writing published occurred in high school as a member of the high school newspaper staff. Beyond that, he kept most of his writing private including an on-and-off journal for about 25 years.

More recently, his public writing has focused on sports, travel, and spirituality/personal growth. Three years ago, Larison started a sports blog where he has found that the most popular posts are stories from his childhood in a reminiscent style similar to the 1980s television sitcom, *The Wonder Years*. In the 90s, he started to write comprehensive trip reports of his family's travel adventures and became a travel agent in 2002. He currently writes about travel on blogs, his company website (**www.familytravelgurus.com**), and various travel discussion forums.

Three years ago, Larison began a spirituality-oriented Twitter account, where he tweeted different quotes that "resonated" with him. He now has more than 4,000 followers on Twitter (**http://twitter.com/calmwithin**). His success with Twitter led him to start a blog by the same name, where he writes about spirituality and life topics.

On **www.calmwithin.com**, Larison posts mainly book reviews. He is part of the Hay House blogger review team (**www.hayhousebooknook. com**), where he has been "one of their most prolific reviewers." He also has received many thank yous and personal recommendations from Hay House's authors, encouraging him to "pursue more writing projects."

Larison gets creative with finding time to write. For journaling, he often writes early in the morning after his daily meditation time. For published writing on blogs, he gets the "creative urge in the evenings, after a busy workday." He will write a first draft, put it aside for the night, and read it the following morning, when he usually will have a few modifications before publishing it.

Drawing from his experience from years of keeping a personal journal, Larison feels his writing is "vulnerable and open." He sees writing as a way to tell the world who he really is. "I enjoy rereading my writing months or years later, as it reminds me what type of person I was at the time and what issues I was dealing with."

For new writers, Larison suggests to "write about what most interests you." He credits *New York Times*' best-selling author, Kathleen Mc-Gowan as saying: "A writer writes!" — a valuable lesson he learned at one of her workshops. Larison has attended various writing workshops given by professional authors and says that each one has had something of value for him.

Larison thinks if you are just starting out as a published author like he is, that "blogging is a good way to start." He feels that the Hay House blogger program is a good way to read a variety of writing styles and get your reviews published. Larison says he has benefited from writing book reviews, as it has exposed him to a variety of writing styles in addition to helping him in honing his own writing skills. He suggests new writers look for opportunities to write guest blogs.

"Don't measure your success by book sales or number of 'hits' to your blog," he says. Instead, ask yourself "Did my words really convey what I was feeling at that moment?" Larison says he has been surprised that some of his most popular book reviews and blog posts were ones he didn't think would get much response, "Yet somehow they resonated with people."

Larison also suggests that writers work on their public speaking skills. Toastmasters®, he says, was a big help to him in this area. "I found once I overcame the public-speaking jitters, my writing skills were a huge help in giving compelling presentations."

Larison is continuing his writing journey and is about to take his next step by writing a book proposal. He is currently researching the differences of "going the self-publishing route versus having an agent."

Chapter 6

A DAY IN THE LIFE

"The reason 99 percent of all stories written are not bought by editors is very simple. Editors never buy manuscripts that are left on the closet shelf at home."

— John Campbell, writer

The primary impetus behind the query is to save time for both the editor and the writer. Editors are bombarded daily with unsolicited manuscripts and articles, which makes it more enticing for them to read a one-page query letter instead of a ten-page story or proposal. Writers submitting a tailored query letter do not waste valuable time or energy preparing a full article that might be rejected. For these two reasons alone, the query letter has become the most effective way for a writer to break into the market and for the editors to acquire the work they need selectively.

The Who, What, and Why of a Query Letter

The query letter is basic. It is a single-page, concise, professional, intriguing letter introducing you and your article idea, story, or book. The query letter serves three clear purposes: 1) gains the editor's attention enough to want to know more about you and your idea, 2) provides an example of your writing skills and style, and 3) outlines your idea and the strategies you plan to use for the full-fledged article.

Who: For beginners and intermediate writers, the query letter is mandatory. Until you have landed regular assignments or have a strong working relationship with an editor, query letters will be your primary means of approaching a publication or editor.

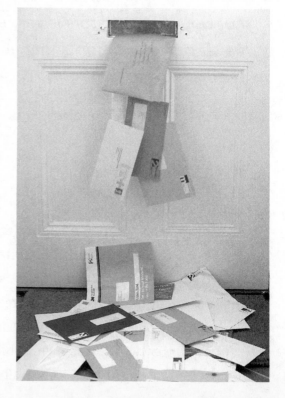

What: The query letter is nothing more than a business letter, a sales pitch of sorts that sells your idea, writing, and qualifications to an editor, agent, or publisher before they have read the entire article or manuscript. Query letters offer a chance for you to make a great first impression without actually being face to face with an editor.

Why: The most obvious and straightforward answer to why use a query letter is editor and agent driven. Editors, agents, and publishers are too busy to read every unsolicited manuscript, article, or proposal that comes across their desks. For practicality sake, the query letter provides a simple solution for managing submissions. One page is much easier to read, skim, and make a first assessment of whether to pursue that writing venture. For writers, the query letter is the best, quickest, and cheapest way to present an idea to a publication without investing too much time and energy for a potential rejection.

Understanding these three questions provides the foundation upon which you will build your skills at query writing. If you are contemplating foregoing the query letter route altogether, think again. The freelance writing market sometimes can be challenging to break into, but by ignoring one of the most important industry rules of querying, you will reduce your chances even further.

Mastering the Art of Querying

Many writers who enter into the publishing arena assume that hard work is the key to success. However, mastering the art of querying is not as much about hard work as it is about work. Yes, the work will be hard at first, but that is primarily because you are learning a new trade. But ultimately, the goal is to work smarter, not harder. The more successful you become at landing assignments, the fewer queries you will need to write. Once you enter this stage, you will find that editors might even start querying you.

Regardless of whether you are just starting out or you have been writing query letters for quite some time, every writer should strive to follow a query "code of ethics." These codes of ethics are not specific details about how to write, develop, or submit the query. They are more relevant to the writer's conduct, for example:

- Always be professional.

- Spend time on the query lead.

- Know the publication and tailor your query accordingly.

- Seek to offer fresh and innovative ideas.

- Do not be shy about being creative in your presentation.

- Provide something interesting such as photos, charts, or diagrams for the editors to look at to add weight to your article.

- Do not propose what you cannot deliver.

- Always provide a brief biography of yourself that shows you are the best person to handle the assignment. Even though you might not have many clips to start with, you can glean from your work experience, personal experience, or a related interview with a subject-matter expert.

Keep this list close at hand whenever you begin a new letter. After a few submissions, these tips will become second nature to you.

CASE STUDY:
RESEARCH AND
KEEP LEARNING

Timothy Patrick
Sneaky Uses for Everyday Things

Timothy Patrick has been a writer for 20 years and has been creating homemade inventions since childhood.

His first introduction to query letter writing began with the purchase of a book about writing book proposals. He studied the query letter writing section, researched potential publishers, and spent a couple of months crafting a great query. All of that research and studying paid off when Patrick landed his first assignment within in two weeks of submitting a query.

Patrick believes query letters work. "Even if a query letter was not necessary, the exercise is important for you to know how to sell your subject," he says. Based on his 20-year experience, Patrick provides these three tips for making a query letter stand out:

- The first paragraph, and especially the first sentence, of your query must be perfect.

- Print out and take your query letter with you to review multiple times a day for at least a couple of weeks.

- Before you complete and submit the query, start writing the article or proposal.

As a technical writer and computer specialist, Patrick understands the importance of finding unique ways to present your ideas. For example, to develop ideas for a good hook, Patrick loves reading feature articles in newspapers and magazines. These resources provide him with just the right inspiration to craft his own interesting and compelling hooks. "It may not be clear where they are going at first, but they take care that the sentences are interesting enough to lead you to the next paragraph where the subject is revealed," expresses Patrick.

If you are just starting out in the writing business, Patrick recommends that you:

- Research your subject. Even if you think you know enough, keep looking up things about it; search the background of other contacts and experts.

- Keep editing your query letters until not a word can be added or omitted.

- Show your work to trusted friends. They point out issues and angles that you may be too involved to see.

Consider the possibilities of alternate media

Like other professional writers, Patrick knows that rejection is inevitable in the querying process. His advice for dealing with the rejections is two-fold: 1) have a list ready of alternate media to submit to and 2) continually evaluate your query ideas and keep submitting them. Patrick is a big fan of exploring other mediums. For example he suggests, "If it is a book idea, submit some of the material as a feature article, a column, a blog post, an MP3 audio, or an e-book." When tailoring your idea to alternate media, Patrick recommends evaluating questions such as:

- Can your idea be turned into a smartphone app?

- Is your idea good material for a TV series episode or movie?

- Can you package your topic (i.e., article or book) with others' ideas?

- Have you tailored your idea for a local, regional, or national market?

When you are excited about a topic and have finally submitted a query, the wait can be frustrating. But Patrick says, "It is important to have other projects out there so your need for feedback is fed. Or, engage in other interests and read more. Inevitably it will lead to more writing project ideas, especially the areas outside your subject."

Some writers have a difficult time imagining that they can be creative when writing query letters. Although you will have to follow protocols when crafting and submitting query letters to editors, agents, and publishers, nothing says you cannot be creative in your presentation.

A common misconception is that the only creativity allowed in writing is in fiction novels or poetry. Writers often think that somehow in these writing genres, the writer is allowed to be more expressive and have more creative liberty. You can add creativity to your query letters by selecting tantalizing words, providing colorful descriptions, adding relevant quotes, and sharing personal anecdotes.

The approach you take in developing the query can easily set you apart from another query from a writer who stuck strictly to the rules by paying close attention to the writer's guidelines and submission instructions. The tone you use in your query can exude creativity, as long as it is appropriate for the publication. The way you present your information in the query, whether in a bulleted or numbered list, a true-false quiz, or bolding and italics for emphasis, can demonstrate your ability to be creative in your approach to communicating your idea or story.

Here are a few essential tips for adding some creative elements to your query letter and increasing your chances of standing out to land an assignment:

- Tailor the content to the publication's mission. After researching the publication, identify the slogan, tagline, or mission statement. Include that somewhere in your letter to show subtly that you have done your homework, and you have become familiar with them.

- Add a thought-provoking quote. Whether it is a quote or a statistic, start your query letter with something that will provoke thought in the reader. Ensure the quote is relevant to the target audiences needs and to the pitch. Adding a quote or statistic is an effective strategy that can attract the attention of an editor, publisher, or agent immediately.

- Add testimonials. Another effective approach for adding creativity to your query letter is to add a testimonial from an industry expert, another author, or a person who has had experience with the topic you are pitching. The purpose of the testimonial is to support the claims you make in your query. It provides additional evidence to why you are the best candidate to handle the assignment.

- Do not forget the P.S. It has been shown that many letter readers start with the postscript section. It is one of the most important elements of a letter, and it draws the most attention. It is not a common element of a query letter, but you can decide if it will add or detract from your query. If you decide to use the P.S. section, make it something important and relevant. Do not waste the reader's time on impertinent information in this section.

- Create your own tagline. Use the skills you learned in Chapter 5 about marketing yourself. Consider a personal slogan or tagline to add to your correspondence (business cards, stationery, website, social media sites, etc.) that will help set you apart from other writers. This will become part of your professional persona and branding strategy; it ultimately will help build and solidify your reputation as a professional writer.

What Else to Include With Your Query

Aside from the standard query letter and self-addressed stamped envelopes (SASE: if you are sending a query to a publisher via snail mail), you may want to add something extra and different for the editor, agent, or publisher to think about. Some of these additions can be considered eye candy to break up the monotony of an editor's engulfing query pile. When crafting your query to a specific publication, consider including the following with it:

- Photos, graphics, and illustrations: Even if you do not have the photos or graphics at the time of submission, it is still a good option to offer to send them as soon as you secure them. You will save the editor valuable time by doing the research to find illustrations, graphics, or photos that would complement your article idea.

- Pull-quotes and sidebars: Recommending sidelights, sidebars, and pull-quotes is a sign that you understand readers. These can function as selling tools or factoids to help the reader gain a quick understanding of the article idea before delving deep into the content. Suggesting these small enhancements sometimes can earn you more money for the article. Remember, it is all about saving the editor time.

- Clips when requested: If a publication request clips, then by all means, send them along. Clips are great way to substantiate your credentials and provide proof that you can do what you say you can do. If an editor tells you not to send clips, and you really want to highlight them in some way, then you can mention them in your query. Just remember to be brief and succinct about it.

These extras sent along with your query can add significant weight and substance. Editors like to have some variety in their day, and what better way to give it to them than by adding a few of these extra special touches to your submission?

Ideally, you are developing a solid image or impression of what it takes to develop a good query letter. Like good writing, a query letter evokes a sense of urgency and clarity. It does not reek of boredom, and yet it gets straight to the business at hand. By now, you understand that the query letter should be a passionate sales pitch that does not overtly send the message that you are either bragging or begging.

A Good Query

For a query letter to be effective, it will need to follow a few basics: It needs to sound interesting; it should never be longer than a page; it should not be about you except when you briefly are stating your credentials; and it should not state the obvious.

Components of the Magazine Article Query

You will not find a magic formula for getting your work published in magazines, but there is an expected format to follow for queries. Use a standard business letter format if the publication requires you to mail your submission. Your name and full contact information should be at the top either centered or right justified. The contact person's full name, title, and contact information should be just below yours, left justified.

This single-page letter uses the following four-paragraph structure:

Paragraph 1: The hook — The hook is an opening paragraph that piques the editor's interest in the idea you are pitching.

Paragraphs 2: Supporting details — The supporting details answers the five W's (who, what, when, where, and why).

Paragraph 3: Qualifications — This paragraph will focus on your qualifications to write the piece you are proposing. It does not have to be lengthy; it merely needs to explain why you are the right person for the assignment.

Paragraph 4: Closing remarks and thank you — Generally considered the closer, this paragraph needs to tie up the loose ends. It should address how soon you can write the piece, and it should mention that you are enclosing a SASE.

Today, most magazine publications allow online submissions via email. In fact, most prefer to be contacted that way. Always check with the specific magazine submission requirements to ensure you are submitting a query in the preferred format. Many jobs have been lost by not following specific guidelines. Always, always, *always* do your research into the publication before submitting.

Querying is a craft, and you will need to discover your own style with words. This process takes time and initiative; it is evolutionary. You must accept the fact that your queries will be rejected, and you will need to be persistent. With each query, strive to learn why it missed the mark and what you can do to improve the next time around.

Components of the Newspaper Query

Thousands if not millions of newspapers are circulating, all of which require a large amount of content. Most of the current staff of these newspapers cannot fulfill the large content requirement, so chances are good that they are accepting submissions from writers, experienced and novice alike. Newspapers reach a far greater audience than most publications, so they are always looking for fresh material every day.

An advantage to querying newspapers is that simultaneous submissions to different newspapers are not frowned upon. The rule of thumb is to submit to newspapers that are 100 miles or more apart. This is because for newspapers, with the exception of national newspapers, running the same or similar article in two different newspapers more than 100 miles away from each other does not cause too much of a threat to the editor and publisher.

The advantage to you as a writer is that you have the potential to make money several times for the same article. That is strategic querying at its best. Additionally, newspaper articles can be used as reprint material for trade publications, magazines, or even books, as long as the information is relevant.

As you have been learning, the first step is to research the publication and study the writer's guidelines. Unfortunately, newspapers rarely have guidelines. But that should not prevent you from picking up the newspaper and dissecting the masthead. The masthead is the section that identifies the editor-in-chief, editor, assistant editor, publisher, staff members, and contributing writers. This information should provide a point of contact for submitting your query. Without writer's guidelines, it can be difficult to know which section to pitch.

Because newspaper articles usually run fewer than 1,000 words, many editors will ask that you send the article along with the query, which means your query letter will function as a cover letter to the article. Some tips when querying for newspapers articles:

- Improve your chances with a local slant. Your chances for publication greatly improve when you write your story for the local audience. This does not apply to national newspapers that are trying to reach as many readers as possible. However, if you are just breaking into the market and have decided to start with your local or regional newspaper, focus on slanting your topic to something that will resonate with local readers. For example, if your specialty is in the food industry, you might suggest an article such as "Five Things You Probably Did Not Know

About Peaches" and recommend running it during the city's annual peach festival.

- Tie it in to a current event. Search the headlines of national and local news to see what types of current events are circulating. Try to tie in your article topic with one of these current events, a particular holiday, or a national event. Use the Internet for research. A host of local and current events can be uncovered.

- Enhance your story with photos. Although photos are not mandatory, they definitely can enhance your story. If you have a decent photo to offer with your pitch, be sure to state that in your query. Do not automatically send in your photo with the query because you most likely will not get it back. When you submit your query, mention that photos are available upon request.

Writing articles for newspapers can be one of the easiest markets to break into. If you are still lacking confidence about submitting query letters to newspapers, you can submit an article to the newspaper's special section that openly solicits readers' stories. These sections are usually the letter to the editor, opinion, parenting, traveling, or personal interest. Once you become comfortable in your local market, look to expand into regional markets and ultimately national markets. All the while, you will be building a strong clip file.

What Editors Really Think of Queries

A love-hate relationship between editors and writers seems to exist. Editors have rules and standards, and writers have the responsibility to follow these rules while also showing creativity, freshness, and simplicity. It seems like a tall order to fill, and yet that is what editors expect. As mentioned, the query letter is an editor's preference over receiving an entire manuscript or fully written article.

Editors, agents, and publishers are bombarded every day with queries, proposals, manuscripts, and other information to read. If you were in that position, what tools would you want to use to help you get through the piles? For editors, queries are one of the most effective tools available to help manage the ideas coming in from countless writers looking to break into the industry.

Publications and the representing editors, agents, and publishers are different. As you work with different publishers, agents, or editors, you will find they all have different opinions, backgrounds, preferences, personalities, and procedures. This is all part of the "art" of querying and working in the writing industry. One of the best skills you can have as a writer, besides the ability to write well, is the ability to listen to the agent, editor, or publisher and determine what works best for each. This will not be an easy task, but it will pay off for you in the end.

Five things that can impress the editor

When you first begin to query, you probably will not know what exactly the editor wants. However, editors are no different from writers in the sense that they are looking for things and ideas that spark interest. Although editors, agents, and publishers have differing opinions, backgrounds, preferences, procedures, and personalities, editors have special tastes when it comes to presentations. Although these five things are not a standard, they will give you an idea of things that can impress an editor. Your job will be to find out what works best for each editor you establish a relationship with. But for now, think about these possibilities:

1. **Let your personality show:** Even though it is only a one-page letter, your personality needs to come across in your query. Editors are looking for personalities that make them chuckle, inspire them, or make them think. Work to make your query letter exude a sense of style and personality. Here is a word of caution though: Try not to sound too casual, gimmicky, or over-the-top. Your goal is to give editors an idea of who you are while maintaining a sense of professionalism.

2. **Have some relevant experience:** This is a difficult angle, particularly for the newbie. With the increasing demands on editors, agents, and publishers, it is refreshing to come across a query letter that shows a writer with experience. That is not to say that a novice cannot land an assignment without experience. It is saying that editors appreciate it when their jobs are made easier. Writers with experience can do that for them.

3. **Be patient:** Inexperienced writers let anxiety get the best of them. Many publications have a long lead time (the time between receiving an assignment and publication of the final piece), and responses often can take up to a month. Editors appreciate it when a writer shows some restraint by not contacting them until a reasonable time has elapsed. Be particularly sensitive to this when the response time is clearly stated in the writer's guidelines.

4. **Show that you have a specialty:** Few writers can write for every topic. Much controversy still exists over whether a writer should specialize or write as a generalist. One can see how from an editor's perspective it would be extremely helpful if the writer had a specialty. Editors, agents, and publishers often already have ideas in mind of what they need. Writers who send in queries and show the editor they have a special knack for the topic of interest more than likely will win the interest of the editor.

5. **Be as perfect as humanly possible:** Editors are definitely not perfect, but somehow you are supposed to be with your submissions. Of course, nobody is perfect, but the expectation is that you need to be as perfect as humanly possible with your query letters and submissions.

The Devil is in the Details

One of the basic skills of querying is to look, act, and sound professional in every way possible. This requires acquiring a command of the rules and paying attention to the details. Think about it from your perspective: What would you think if you received a five-page packet addressed to the wrong person, with blatant spelling errors on canary yellow paper? Would that make you want to contact that person right away, or would that make you cringe in disgust? This is what editors, agents, and publishers deal with on a daily basis.

Writers abound who believe that the details should be overlooked because we are human and mistakes happen. However, it is within your control to put your best foot forward and make a lasting impression. So, what exactly are these details? Take a look:

- **Know whom to address and how:** Even though staff assistants will most likely forward your query to the right department, do not use that as an excuse to not address the right person. Do your research to find out to whom you should submit your query. This small detail will show the editor you can do your homework, and you will go the extra distance. Try not to make gender assumptions. For example, if you are sending a query to a women's magazine, do not assume the editor will be a woman. Also, if you are unsure of the gender of the editor whose name could be either a male or female, call the publication to get clarification or do some digging on the Internet. This does not just apply to names. It is professional not only to know whom to address but also to know the person's correct title.

- **Format to industry standards:** There is really no excuse for writers to have query letters formatted in a substandard manner. Typewriters and handwritten queries are no longer acceptable because they clue the editor to the fact that the writer has not written much, or even lately. Clean, smudge-free, white paper is professional. Nowadays, email submissions are the standard. Check the writer's guidelines to determine if they have specific formatting guidelines. It might be tempting to add a little creativity to your formatting, but you will need to refrain until you land the assignment and get to know the editor, agent, or publisher better.

- **Include a SASE:** If you are sending a query by snail mail, the professional thing to do is send a self-addressed stamped envelope along with it. Only an amateur does not include a SASE, so remembering this detail will differentiate your submission from theirs. One of your goals as a writer is to show the editor that you intend to make it as easy as possible for him or her. A good way to demonstrate this is by including a SASE, especially because no company is going to pay postage to send you a rejection. Also consider this: Sending a SASE with every query can get expensive. Unfortunately, it is part of the protocol, so be sure to budget for it in your business expenses.

- **Address the publication correctly:** It is getting more challenging to identify the correct address of a publication or publishing house. Many of the larger organizations have multiple addresses, and some of those addresses are even international. Use the Internet and the writer's guidelines to determine the correct address and name of the company to which you are submitting your query. This detail often irritates the editor and will label your query a waste of time. If you are not willing to take the time to pay attention to the details of the address of the publication you are submitting the query to, can the editor really expect you to pay attention to the details when you are writing an article slotted for publication?

- **Proofread, proofread, proofread:** Double and triple-check your query, particularly for spelling errors, grammatical mistakes, typos, and incorrect facts. These imperfections signal to the editor that you lack professionalism and are not willing to spend extra time doing things right.

Here are a few tips to help you ensure you have an error-free query letter:

- **Sleep on it.** One of the best techniques for dealing with the details of your query is to let it stew overnight and come back to it the next day with a fresh perspective. You will be amazed at the number of things you notice with a good night's rest.

- **Get help from a friend.** Enlist the help of a friend to read your query letter. Often a fresh set of eyes from an unbiased person can pick up typos, inconsistencies, and other errors you might not have noticed yourself.

- **Read aloud.** Either have someone else read your letter aloud or read it aloud to yourself. This exercise often identifies unclear statements or thoughts and poor grammar or sentence structure.

- **Look up the rules.** Proofreading can be easier with the help of a handbook or style. If a phrase does not seem right or you are not sure about punctuation, look it up in common stylebooks such as *AP Stylebook* or the *Chicago Manual of Style*.

- **Read bottom to top.** Our brains get used to nonexistent letters, words, and punctuation, which allow us to skip over what would otherwise be blatant errors. To trick your natural tendency, read your query letter from the bottom up. Also, try reading the text in a sentence backward, which breaks up the rhythm and flow of your writing. This approach helps your brain focus on the letters and words.

- **Focus on punctuation.** Uncover errors in sentence structure by focusing on the punctuation in your query letter. Circle every instance of punctuation: comma, period, semicolon, colon, quotation marks, etc. If you are working in a word-processing program, bold or highlight all punctuation.

- **The spell-checker feature in your word processing program can help, but it is not foolproof.** With the increasing acceptance of typos and grammatical errors, taking the time to fix the mistakes in your query letter is essential now more than ever. A clean, properly written, edited piece projects a professional image and will go a long way to ensure you are taken seriously in the world of writing and publishing.

The Anatomy of a Query Letter

From an editor's perspective, query letters come in all shapes, sizes, and colors. Some are amusing, others are amateurish, and even more find a home in the slush pile. A good query letter, one that can grab an editor's attention quickly provides a writer with the possibility of future assignments and a long-term, profitable relationship.

Greetings and salutations

The salutation sets the tone for the rest of the letter. Look at the following salutation scenarios to see the message the editors receive when you are not careful with your greetings and salutations.

If your salutation addresses the wrong gender, "Dear Mr. Jamie Benson" [Jamie is a woman], then the editor knows you did not dig deep enough to find out if Jamie was a man or woman. If you did not research this one small point, how will you research information to substantiate your claims in an assigned article? If your salutation addresses the person incorrectly or you spell the person's name wrong, the editor will know that you are not willing to pay attention to the details. If you do not take the time to proof your one-page letter, will you take the time to proof your article before submitting it for publication?

If your salutation reads, "Dear Sir or Madam:" then the editor knows you are too lazy to figure out to whom to address the query. If you are too lazy to look up a point of contact, then chances are you probably will not meet the article deadline.

If your salutation is too relaxed, "Hey Pam," then the editor knows that you are probably not going to be professional in your future dealings.

Aside from the address, the salutation is the first line of the official query. If you get that wrong, the rest is downhill from there.

Make it a good closer

On the opposite side of the salutation is the closing statement. How you close your letter also sends a specific message to the editor. If you do not have a rapport with an editor, agent, or publisher, it is best to go with a more generic, professional closing rather than a more relaxed closer. Take a look:

"Sincerely yours,"
"Take care,"

"Goodbye,"

"Respectfully,"

"Warmest regards,"

"Godspeed,"

"Regards,"

"Cheers,"

"Later, alligator,"

"Best regards,"

"Best wishes,"

"Peace,"

"Kind regards,"

"Hope to hear from you soon,"

"Talk to you later,"

"Cordially,"

"Looking forward to your response,"

"Shine on,"

You can use plenty of other closing statements, but with the ones demonstrated above, you have an idea of how to send the right message with your closer. Now that you are familiar with the bookends of the query letter, it is time to dive into the specific elements of the query.

Five core sections of a query letter

At the core of this small, yet powerful, one-page letter are five main sections. The first three sections will discuss the piece you are pitching. The last two sections will cover talking about yourself and establishing a rapport with the decision maker. This chapter breaks down each of these sections so you can learn the purpose of each and how to successfully develop each section so at the end you have a solid and irresistible query letter.

Section One: Now that I have your attention (The Hook)

Is it the hook or the lead? The answer: It is both or either. Many people reference the opening paragraph as the lead. Others just refer to it as the hook because that is what you are trying to do: hook the reader. If there is one place in your query where it is worth investing your time, it is best to spend it crafting the hook. The hook should be a concise, one- to two-sentence tagline for your entire piece. It is intended to captivate the reader's interest and motivate them to ask for more. Use these first few lines to prove that you are a skilled writer and have a saleable idea.

You can approach the hook in several ways; the following are just a few of these commonly used techniques:

- **Solve a problem.** Start your query by defining a problem or situation that is common to the audience of the publication you are addressing. Next, propose a piece that will solve that problem.

- **Use the Five W's:** Who, what, where, when, why. Although this approach can often result in a dry question and answer banter, it functions as a good rule for starting a query.

- **Use the inverted pyramid.** This technique is another valued aid for structuring your hook. The concept is simple: Start with strong points first and end with the details. Trying to tell a story at first will lose the reader's interest. Start strong with an attention-grabbing statement or question and then develop the main points later.

- **Provide useful information.** When using this approach, start by presenting two to three lines of pertinent information (i.e., statistics, facts, figures, etc.). Then close the hook by explaining how your proposed piece is relevant to the target audience.

- **Use a quote.** Begin your query letter with a saying or quote from a famous person or expert in the field. A good strategy is to obtain a quote from a subject-matter expert, prominent figure, or person with first-hand experience in your subject.

- **Add a personal touch.** Anecdotes can be a solid hook for an editor. Many well-established writers like to use this approach because it immediately establishes credibility by experience. However, proceed with caution when you add a personal touch. First, ensure the publication uses a more relaxed tone for the targeted audience. If they do not, you want a more professional style.

- **Provide shock value.** The goal with this approach is to make the reader sit up and pay attention. Maybe you want to provide something bizarre or so unbelievable that it makes the editor, agent, or publisher want to request more simply out of curiosity.

- **Compare and contrast.** Do a comparison of how two companies are using a technique or product to provide a solution to their end users.

Things to avoid in the hook

Take heed and avoid these common hooks, which are most often submitted by amateur writers:

- **Too personal:** Stay away from hooks that introduce yourself ("Hi, my name is Sally, and I would like to submit this letter for your review...") or provide too much or irrelevant information. ("I am a long-time fan of the Grateful Dead, and much of their music inspired my writing career...")

- **Brownnosing:** Do not just give lip service to an editor. They want evidence by your writing style, your attention to detail, and your ability to follow through on your assignments. Avoid brownnosing and "kissing up" to the editor. ("I have an entire bookshelf full of issues of this magazine; I have been a subscriber almost all my adult life.")

- **The sympathy angle:** If you have never been published before, the editor will not care, and chances are, they might even discard your letter just because you tried to pull the sympathy card. ("Even though I have never been published before, I know I can do a good job with this assignment.") Stick to what you know, present a clear, concise, professional letter, and you will get a lot farther.

- **The perfect fit:** Everyone thinks they are the perfect fit when trying to land an assignment. Even though you might be a good fit for the article, avoid singing your own praises. ("I would be a perfect fit for this because I have the right experience and credentials for your magazine.") Again, editors want proof with a good query, substantiating facts, and supporting credentials.

- **I am just an amateur:** You might be an amateur, but no one else needs to know about it. Do not call attention to your lack of writing experience or your lack of credentials. Write your query letter in a manner that makes the editor want your work regardless of your experience.

You can use numerous hook techniques to pique an editor's interest. Study samples of successful queries and learn why those hooks worked. Then get to work crafting your own successful hook.

Section Two: Here is my story (The Pitch)

Once you land the hook, now it is time to make the pitch. The pitch is where you explain what exactly it is you are proposing. Editors want to know a little bit about how the piece will work in the publication. This is a good time to show the editor you have thought this through.

Now that you have told the editor what you intend to write, this is where you demonstrate what you intend to write about it. Here are a few ways you can show how you plan to cover your topic:

- **State the purpose.** Approach this pitch with a lead-in such as, "This article will focus on helping career-minded women develop their own brands." Or "The goal of my book is to provide step-by-step, visual instructions on how to build a birdhouse like the pros." Putting these types of statements early in the pitch ensures you have conveyed your subject and slant clearly.

- **Outline your plan of attack.** A good rule is to choose three to six interesting topics you will cover and write a couple of sentences for each topic. Try to avoid the standard school outline format; it shows unprofessionalism and lack of creativity. Instead, use bulleted or numbered lists or indented paragraphs to create a sense of hierarchy and order.

- **Prove it with numbers.** There is no better way of validating your claims than to provide the facts from a reliable source. For example, your query can include something like, "The recently published a study confirming that the percentage of overweight Americans has gone from 30 percent to 35 percent in the last five years," and your credibility has just increased twofold.

The purpose of the pitch is to explain clearly why you are proposing this idea and how you intend to develop the story so the targeted audience can benefit from it. What you discuss in your pitch will be dictated somewhat by the publication to which you are querying. How you develop your pitch will be the difference between the top of the heap or the slush pile.

Section Three: In case you need more detail (The Body)

This is the meat and potatoes of the letter. This section is where the selling begins. If query letters and creativity converge, this is the place. In section three, you want to develop your idea further to provide enough detail for the editor, agent, or publisher to get an idea of where you are going with your proposed work. Your support details can come in a variety of shapes and sizes, but most of them will fall into one of the following categories:

- A good way to substantiate your story is to provide facts, figures, and statistics. Citing some relevant facts provides good evidence and supports your claims.

- Interviewing relevant, well-respected experts is a great way to establish credibility with the editor and ultimately with the readers of the publication.

- Reuse the anecdotal approach in the summary section. They are just as effective here, but now you can add more detail.

- Creating a reference point for your subject can be an effective way to provide context to your idea. Predictions of the importance of this topic in the near or distant future can be a strong selling point.

- A good strategy is to try to tie your piece in with a seasonal event such as Christmas, Fourth of July, National Doughnut Day, or Take Your Daughter to Work Day.

- You also can use this section to detail things like word count (rounding to the nearest 500), to which issue the piece should be tailored, and a working title. Before confidently stating the word counts, be sure to check the publication's guidelines to confirm the average length of pieces they require. Be flexible about your title. State that this is a proposed or working title because editors, agents, and publishers frequently change titles.

- Maybe you do photography on the side or know someone who is a good illustrator. At the time of the query, you do not have to have visual aids ready or included, but if you can state that you can secure photos or provide diagrams or illustrations, that will add weight to your pitch. Describe in as much detail as space will permit the type of visual aids you can provide. The visual aid is important to the content. The goal is best conveyed by using a caption. If you do not intend to provide visual aids, you definitely can provide suggestions. The editor, agent, or publisher will be happy to know that you have taken time to think through how the final piece might work.

The creativity should be demonstrated in your writing style, how you intended to present the material using bulleted lists, call-out boxes, quizzes, spin-offs, and subsequent subtopics. If after you have developed your summary, you find that you have more than one page of descriptive information, your query is probably too long. It may be necessary for you to use that length to develop the supporting details, but keep this in mind: Editors are busy; they would prefer not to have to read more than one page.

A strong, well-crafted summary is the heart of your effective sales piece. Once you have gone through your details, edit it down to remove wordy phrasing, clichés, awkward sentences, and impertinent information. You can be creative with your summary, but do not overdo it and lose the essence of your idea.

Section Four: The ideal candidate (The Credentials)

As you have learned in previous chapters, editors, agents, and publishers want to know why you are the best person to handle the assigned project. Whatever you do, do not lie or cover up your qualifications. This will be a bad career move and often can be difficult to recover from. You do not have to be modest in your query letter. You do not want to come across sounding arrogant or as a braggart, but there is nothing wrong with boasting a bit to show that you can do the job.

A good approach to this section is to start by writing a biography. This is a good exercise because you can write it once and then craft smaller versions of it for each query. To ensure you are putting your best foot forward, try a few of these tactics:

Use a little bit of life: Start with your education or professional experience as a way to gather credentials. If either of these is related to your pitch, they can be used to substantiate the claims you make in your query. For example, if you write content for the company newsletter, provide technical content for business proposals, or write copy for the corporate website, these are examples of a writing background. If you write any material that possibly could connect to the query topic, include photocopies with your query.

Any degree, even if it is not related to your query topic, can provide credibility in your bio. If you attended relevant courses or obtained a license or certification that pertains to the topic of your query, be sure to include that as well. Writing courses should be excluded because they can potentially emphasize your lack of writing experience. Instead, mention courses you have taken to enhance your understanding of the topic you are pitching. Any teaching or speaking you have done could prove interesting to editors. Another way to use a little bit of life is to add life experiences, either your own or someone else's. Life experience can add depth to your story and a feeling of authenticity.

Emphasize the positive: Instead of calling attention to your lack of writing clips or your previous rejections, work toward making a more positive impression. Do not use language that will emphasize your shortcomings. Instead, rework the language in your query letter to stress more of what you have done rather than what you have not done.

For example, if you are submitting a query to a book publisher and you do not have any book credits, list magazine or newspaper credits if you have them. If you do not have any publishing credits to offer, focus on crafting your credentials to emphasize years of experience in the topic you are presenting. Do an honest assessment of what you bring to the table, and find a way to present it in the best possible fashion so you can show your strengths as a writer.

Use the right endorsements: Having your family, colleague, or best friend endorse your work will not impress an agent, publisher, or editor. Of course, if Stephen King happens to be your uncle and he recommends your work, your chances have just improved. Nevertheless, if you can acquire just the right endorsement, it can give your query the added leverage you need to get the reader's attention. Endorsements are more commonly recommended for book queries than article

queries. So, if you can include the right endorsement, you can enhance your query.

Who is the best endorser for your query? First, that will depend upon the topic you are pitching. If your book project is about health and fitness, then it would be ideal to gather an endorsement from Jillian Michaels.

Although third-party, expert, or famous endorsements might be hard to solicit, you also can enhance your query by getting an existing client, previous boss, or former teacher to refer you and your work. Think of it as providing references during a job search. In either case, be sure to have the endorser's full and complete permission to use his or her name and reference or quote.

Honors and awards: If you have been recognized for outstanding performance or other relevant achievements, this is a good place to include that information. Carefully pick the honors and awards that are important and add weight to the topic you are pitching in your query letter. Touting an award for "IT Training Specialist of the Year" will not impress an editor, publisher, or agent if your topic is about making a career change. On the other hand, if you are writing a book about the benefits of training and certification in the information technology field, then your award becomes relevant. It quickly can establish you as an expert on that topic. Consider the letter you are pitching, think of the audience that will be reading the article or book, and start pulling together accolades that match or complement that subject.

Professional and social memberships: Another valuable way to enhance your credibility is to add your participation in professional and social organizations. This credential functions as another way to establish you quickly as an expert.

Media and publicity: If you want to make an editor, agent, or publisher happy, show that you are promotable. If you can show you have experience with personal appearances through radio, newspapers, magazines, television, speaking engagements, or teaching, this can work to your advantage. The more often you get your name out and heighten your profile, the better impression you can make on editors, publishers, and agents.

After you have gathered all the pieces together and drafted a preliminary bio, edit it down to one paragraph. If you have an extensive background, two paragraphs will do. Do not be discouraged if you do not have credentials starting out. You can gain relevant qualifications from a variety of sources, including professional experience, academic training and background, teaching experience, expert interviews, and personal experience. Just start working toward your goal, and the credentials will come.

Do not forget this most important element: Before ending your query with the closing statement, be sure you include a paragraph thanking the editor for his or her time and consideration. Most editors greatly appreciate this small attention to detail and are surprised how many writers miss this part in the query. A sign of appreciation can yield big results.

Section Five: Some parting thoughts (The Closer)

Be professional and respectful. Ideally, you have been getting that message loud and clear as you dissect the contents of these chapters. The purpose of this last section of the query letter is to thank the editor, agent, or publisher for reviewing your proposal. You also can use it to offer one last attempt to encourage the reader to respond and let them know you have provided a SASE for that convenience.

Never make the editor work harder than he or she already does. Have your contact information easily accessible so the editor knows exactly how he or she can follow up with you. Include a brief reference to any clips you have included. If you have a website, make it highly visible. And above all else, be professional and respectful.

Tailored for Success: Editors are used to seeing the same ideas pitched query after query. Then, your query pops up with an idea that seems similar, but you have taken extra special care to delve deeper into the idea and tailor it specifically for what you think the publication needs or the reader would like to know. You have captivated the editor, and your article most likely will be published. How did this happen? Well, you most likely:

- Demonstrated that you understand the publication's requirements

- Detailed how your idea would be a good fit for that particular publication

- Researched past articles

- Illustrated how your writing style is similar to the publication's

Attention to the details is what can set your query apart from the rest. Tailoring is a technique that experienced writers use to demonstrate to the editor that they have done the research.

Whether you are writing a query for an article, nonfiction book, or novel or are writing to an agent, do not stray from this basic anatomy. Developing your own set of rules for a query format will not impress an editor, publisher, or agent. Play by the rules, be professional, and write a good piece. Before you know it, you will find yourself one step closer to a sale.

The query is not a résumé or a rambling tome of your writing life. It is a simple, one-page letter introducing you and your work. Keep it simple and stick to the basic anatomy.

Chapter 7

MAKING A LIVING WRITING

"Any man who keeps working is not a failure. He may not be a great writer, but if he applies the old-fashioned virtues of hard, constant labor, he'll eventually make some kind of career for himself as writer."

— Ray Bradbury, author

Where to Find Writing Jobs

Got lots of ideas, but no idea where to start looking for writing jobs? There is a market for almost every topic you can think of, so do not feel like you are limited. Between newspapers, trade magazines, e-zines, consumer magazines, and literary journals, your options are endless for writing jobs.

There are many ways to discover markets that are open to hiring freelance writers. Finding places to submit your work is easy, as long as you know where to look. Here are some suggestions of where to look:

- *The Writer's Market* is an absolute go-to source for writing. An online version available at **www. writersmarket.com** is continually updated.

- *Absolute Markets* puts out a biweekly newsletter with both U.S. and International market guidelines. **www. absolutemarkets.com**

- *Writer's Digest* has a searchable database of markets at **www.writersdigest.com.**

- *Funds For Writers* is a weekly listing of jobs, contests, and grants for writers at **www.fundsforwriters.com.**

- *The bookstore:* Head to the bookstore and peruse the magazine section to get an idea of the host of magazine topics out there.

- *The Internet:* Hit the Internet and search for publication options by topic of interest. Want to write about bears in New England? I bet there is a magazine or online source where you can do just that. But, you will not know it if you do not do your research.

The key to finding writing jobs is to understand your target market.

1. Audience: Does my article fit the audience in this market? Does the audience fit my topic?

2. Market: Does my idea or topic work best in one particular market over another? Can I cross over markets?

3. Fit: Does the market or publication publish my type of idea or topic?

4. Acceptance: Does the market accept freelance work, beginners, or established writers?

5. Payment: Does the market or publication pay? How well? If they do not pay, what do they offer the writer for compensation?

Targeting your Submissions

Successful freelance writers have learned to target their submissions to the publication they are sending it in to. As a result, they are able to land publication after publication. In order to target your submissions, you must follow the publication's guidelines exactly. Anything less is considered unprofessional.

The guidelines are the rules of the publication. The primary purpose is to help writers determine whether they want to approach the publication and how. Depending on the source you use, writer's guidelines can vary. Fortunately, most guidelines contain basically the same information; it just may be presented in a different order with details specific to that publication.

To give you an idea of what to expect, the following elements are good examples of publication guidelines to research before querying a publication:

- **Point of contact:** You are looking for the person to whom to send the query. Some entries include the publisher and editor at the beginning and then provide another name as the point of contact. When you are not sure to whom you should submit the query, look at the masthead of the publication, and query the assistant editor or someone comparable.

- **How to contact:** Mail, fax, or email: Which one is the best way to send your query? Do not assume every editor would gladly accept an email submission. Look to the guidelines to be sure. If it is not specified, then default to either fax or email to save on postage costs. Not only is this section about how to submit the query, but it also indicates whether to submit a query or a complete manuscript. If the guidelines do not specify either way, be safe and send a query.

- **Type of material accepted:** Read this section carefully. Publications often will list the various types of materials they do not accept rather than what they will accept. This is a guideline that if followed can set you apart from the competition.

- **Percentage of freelance material accepted:** You want to look for publications that have a high percentage of freelance material, usually about 80 percent or more. This means your chances of getting accepted are higher than publications with a lower percentage. You still can query publications with lower freelance acceptance percentages; it just means your chances of securing an assignment are reduced significantly.

- **Publication frequency:** It is important to know how often the publication publishes an issue. You want to ensure your query is relevant to a particular topic, season, or issue. Knowing the frequency of a publication allows you present a timely query, which shows the editor you are familiar with the publication.

- **Pay rates:** On average, and at a glance, you can get a feel for what the publication pays. Become familiar with the two types of payment terms, which are "pays upon acceptance" and "pays upon publication."

- **Payment terms:** If you have the option to negotiate this, choose pays upon acceptance because, typically, you will receive payment sooner. Acceptance means the editor likes your article and will use when it comes time for publication, which can happen several weeks to months later.

- **Rights purchased:** This section details whether the publication will own the rights of the piece once submitted, if the rights expire after a certain amount of time, or if the writer retains all rights to the work. If you are unfamiliar with terms used in this section, you will need to research them carefully in order to understand fully the rights you are selling to the publisher.

- **Photo submissions:** Submitting photos with your query can improve your chances of acceptance, but only if you follow the publication guidelines. This section provides specific details on how to and what kind of photos to submit including photo size, resolution, rights, and format.

- **Columns or departments:** Review several copies of the publications you intend to query. You might notice that many of the publications divide the content into several columns and departments. Check this section carefully to see if a particular column or department accepts freelance pieces. The column you wanted to pitch to might be slotted for a regular industry expert.

- **Editor's notes:** If you want some more hints on how to approach an editor, spend time reading the editor's notes. This will help you tailor your query even more or it can help you rule out the publication before spending time developing the query.

- **Byline or bio credits:** A byline or bio credit provides additional credibility for your clip file and is another way for you to promote your business, products, or services.

Although bylines are commonplace, confirm that the publication offers a byline or bio; it can enhance your prestige and add to your credentials when submitting queries.

- **Lead time:** This time will vary greatly depending on the size of the publication and circulation. The larger the publication, the longer the lead time, which is the amount of time an editor needs to review manuscripts for a specific issue. For example, there usually will be a cutoff date for submitting manuscripts intended for a particular month. For query letters, it is best to try to submit your ideas well in advance of the publication's editorial calendar, particularly if your topic is seasonal.

- **Acceptance of simultaneous submissions:** You are engaging in simultaneous submissions (SimSubs) when you query several agents, editors, or publishers at the same time. Some publications refuse to review your query if they know it is a simultaneous submission. It often can create confusion and complications when it comes time for publication. Be careful about the publications that accept simultaneous submissions. Say you submitted your work to two publications and one publication wants to publish your piece. Unfortunately, you have already agreed to have it published with the other publication or the publication already ran the piece. Simultaneous submissions can make it difficult for you to refuse an editor. When you sent out simultaneous submissions, you most likely will offer exclusive rights to the publication that accepts your topic. If more than one publication wants to use your piece, you will have to choose which one, and withdraw your submission from the others. It also makes it harder for an editor to secure new ideas from you. Inadvertently, you have created a more competitive environment, which can discourage editors. Writers and editors have had differing opinions on SimSubs for decades. For writers, simultaneous submissions offer the increased chance of getting your work published quicker. However, most editors do not like simultaneous submissions for the simple reason that they make their buying decision based on how a piece will fit in with a specific theme for an issue. Once the editor makes plans for a story, they do not like the idea that a piece is now unavailable because it has been sold to someone else.

- **Requesting a sample copy:** Whether the publication provides a free sample copy or not, you will need to send a self-addressed, stamped envelope (SASE) along with your request. Publications will not pay the postage to send you a sample copy. Check this section carefully because many publications charge a fee for sample copies. If the publication has a website, check to see if you can find a sample copy there, and spare yourself the postage.

- **Kill fee:** A kill fee is not as bad as it sounds. It can be an advantage for you, especially because you put the time and effort into finishing the assignment. A kill fee generally represents 25 to 50 percent of the original payment promised. This is what you would receive if the article you wrote was scheduled to be published but then got canceled. If the article was canceled, the writer receives the kill fee regardless of whether the payment was on acceptance or publication.

- **Response time:** A good piece of information to know after you submit your query is how long you will have to wait before hearing the news. Similar to lead times, response times will vary depending on the publication size. The larger the publication, the longer the response time. If you have not heard back from the publication after the response time has elapsed, it is OK to follow up.

- **Acceptance of reprints:** The use of reprints is specific to each publication. Reprints are advantageous for the writer, but some publications do not use them at all. Although the price for reprints is dramatically reduced from the original fee, it still can be a profitable outlet because you do not have to do any rewriting.

- **Word counts:** If a publication has different departments, they might require varying word counts. You easily can determine the average word count for each section of the publication by investigating a few issues. Generally, feature articles can run between 1,000 and 6,000 words, editorials between 500 and 750.

- **General information:** This is a great section to reference when you want to learn more about the publication. It often can shed some light on what the publication is all about without you having to purchase a copy from the library, newsstand, or send off for a sample copy.

- **Founding date:** The longer the publication has been around, the better your chances are for getting an assignment. That is not to say newly established publications do not provide opportunity. Unfortunately, many new publications have to deal with the reputation of underpaying freelancers or not paying at all. It is a generalization, but often, the more established publications are typically more stable and pose less risk for you.

- **Circulation:** This is the number of readers a potential advertiser could reach by advertising in the publication. This number is important to you because it can indicate a couple of things: It can help you determine whether the publication is regional or national, and it can give you an idea of pay rate and prestige.

Do not let this list overwhelm you. The more familiar you become with the terminology, the easier it will be for you find what you are looking for. Writer's guidelines exist to increase your chances of getting published because editors can easily weed out the writers who submit queries that do not follow guidelines. Another reason these guidelines exists is to prevent you from wasting your time. It takes more time to try to mind read a publication's needs than it does to look up and follow the instructions.

If your idea has not been successful in one market, then try another.

CASE STUDY:
DO SOMETHING
WRITING-RELATED EVERY DAY

Kevin Sheehan
Email: huntersheal@gmail.com
Web: www.huntershea.com

"If you can't be a rock star, be a writer! Never give up. I repeat: never… give…up. You will succeed if you keep working." Kevin Sheehan

Kevin Sheehan has been writing for nearly 20 years, two of those years as a professional. He considered himself more than a beginner, but not quite an expert. Kevin has written magazine articles, book reviews, Web page content, online articles, newsletters, fliers, blogs, and is the author of a handful of books. He considers writing his night and weekend job and confesses that it does require more of his time with each passing year.

"I've been writing in multiple genres, with a concentration in horror fiction, for almost two decades now. What started out as a hobby or diversion has turned into a second career and an absolute obsession," Kevin says.

Back in the mid-90s, around the time *The X Files* was getting its start, Kevin was in a terrible, dead-end job.

"I happened to notice that the guy sitting next to me, who was rapidly becoming a good friend, was writing a novel. This blew me away. I thought people who wrote novels were either recluses or professors. What did I know? He inspired me to start writing, which at first was a great creative outlet and a way to escape the everyday stress of life. Funny thing was, once I got started, I couldn't stop."

"I began by writing short stories (most of them horrible) and got my first acceptance at a paying online magazine. That was followed up by a novel (a romantic comedy) that I self-published, followed by two more novels that were picked up by a very small publisher. It didn't pay much, but it was satisfying to see my work in print!"

Over the years, writing has become a true passion and something Kevin can't imagine not doing. Recently, things have taken a turn for the better, he says, proof that you should never give up. For inspiration, Kevin tattooed "never give up" on his arm to commemorate his recent contract signings.

"I just love creating whole worlds and characters and letting the story take me on a ride. I don't do outlines, and my books never, ever end the way I initially thought they would. The story determines the outcome and I love that surprise that seems to leap from my subconscious onto the page. You'll often hear me stop and say, "Wow, I didn't see that coming." I also enjoy the marketing of my work, specifically the social media tools that allow me to connect and interact with readers. I've met some amazing folks that way. Heck, I even had a fan that runs a microbrewery name a lager after one of my books. That was an awesome moment."

Kevin does something writing-related just about every single day; whether it's writing something new, revisions, marketing, blogging, submissions, you name it. He typically works in the early evening after putting in a full day's work at his "day job."

"If I'm in the middle of a big project like a novel, I try to put in at least one to two hours a day until the first draft is complete, and then let it sit and rise like dough for a few weeks."

He's not one of those people who says you have to write every day.

"Life often gets in the way. But, always have something you're working on and set attainable goals for yourself. If you have a busy week, that goal may be 2,000 words. On a light week, ratchet it up to 10,000 words. Best way to amp up your writing: Cut down on TV. Watching TV is a time drag. If you cut your time in front of the tube in half, you won't believe how much time you'll have to write."

The *Writer's Market* is his "bible." Kevin used their online version to find markets, agents, and publishers looking for work. Now that Kevin has an agent, she does a lot of that legwork for him, but he still uses professional contacts, networking at conferences, and genre-specific associations to find magazines looking for stories and articles.

Querying is just part of the job, he says. "If I've completed something that's ready to be sent out, I'll spend a night a week looking for 'homes' and sending out query letters."

"At this point, I only query if I'm looking for a place to send a short story to, but since most of my concentration has been on books, I'm happy to have my agent on hand to do that. Luckily, I have an amazing agent."

First and foremost, Kevin says, any aspiring writer needs to read, read, read.

"The more you read, the better your writing will be. You'll also learn along the way which publishers showcase the type of writing you want to pursue, who the editors and agents are, and the trends in the market. The *Writer's Market* is an invaluable tool, especially at the start of your career. You also need to get out and network. Find organizations that match your genre (for example, the Horror Writers Association for folks like me) and join them. Go to conventions. Don't be shy. Talk to everyone you can, pick their brains, find out who is looking for what. As an example, I recently went to a horror convention that features not only writers but also actors, directors, you name it. I went to a panel discussion of authors and ran into one of them later in the day. We struck up a conversation and talked all about the industry and books like a couple of old friends. Turns out, he also worked for a publisher that I had been dying to work with for over a decade. He asked me to send him something and that turned into a sale for an anthology. I wouldn't have gotten that sale if I hadn't gone to that convention, actively sought him out, and introduced myself."

Kevin currently has two horror novels coming out with Samhain Publishing (*Forest of Shadows* and *Evil Eternal*), as well as stories in various horror magazines and anthologies.

"I lead a double writing life, thanks to my agent who sold a picture book I had written for my children to Schwartz & Wade, a division of Random House. I'm busy working on more picture books as well as a horror/adventure series for all those kids who can't get enough of Goosebumps. It's been a bumpy, crazy ride, but worth ever minute of it."

Writing for Newspapers

Writing for newspapers can be another good way to jump-start your writing career, and the payoff can be great once you have landed a few assignments. The best place to get started with newspaper writing is in your market. The key to breaking into this market involves a combination of the following:

- **Persistence:** Persistence is the key when querying your ideas to the editor. Do not take it personally because editors receive hundreds of queries weekly, sometimes daily if it is a larger circulation.

- **Reliability:** Newspapers work against tight deadlines and have a daily requirement for new, fresh, or up-to-the-minute content. You do not always need to be extra creative or have the most technically sound content. Those who submit on time, on topic, and within the allotted space requirements do the best.

- **Contacts:** This industry is built around your contact list. If you are new to the industry, start networking to build your circle of influence. A phone call or a brief email to the editor of your local or regional paper could open up a world of opportunities. The amount of time it takes to make a connection will well be worth it in the end.

Here are a few other things to remember if you decide to pursue the newspaper market: Listen, observe, get in the field, and engage in the human experience as much as possible.

Writing for Magazines

Writing for magazines is the market most writers try to break into. Observe the checkout at any local supermarket or convenience store, waiting rooms in doctor and dentist offices, airplanes, hotels, and health clubs. The selection of consumer magazines is endless.

The consumer magazine world has a language and protocol of its own. If you do not master the language and follow the protocol, you will run into many obstacles, which will lead to unnecessary frustration. To increase your odds of getting an assignment, become familiar with the publications you want to solicit. For each magazine of interest to you, study and focus on the following five areas: audience, market, article topic, freelance acceptance, and payment.

After you have studied the magazine and clearly answered those five areas, write to the publication for their writer's guidelines. Many magazines now have online versions and post writer's guidelines online. Start your search on the Web first, and if you cannot find it there, you will need to submit a letter asking for guidelines and enclose a SASE for the response.

Literary Magazines

Unlike consumer magazines, a literary magazine (also known as a literary journal), such as *The New Yorker, The Atlantic, Harper's Magazine*, and the *Harvard Review*, is a publication that focuses strictly on creative writing with an emphasis on projecting a "literary" feel. These magazines are often affiliated with a university or independent literary publisher.

Getting your fiction story or poetry published might be challenging, but it is possible. Although this market struggles to pay substantially, most writers submit for the prestige and look to publishing in literary magazines as a way to jump-start a career in fiction writing. The good news is that literary magazines often welcome and encourage submissions from new writers.

With literary magazines, starting small might be your best bet. Look first at colleges and universities because circulation through these avenues is usually low and regional. This type of publication generally is looking for scholarly essays, stimulating prose, book reviews, poetry, and sometimes art and photography.

The key to success in this area is to present yourself as a professional and have a system in place for submissions. As with consumer magazine articles, the first step to getting your fiction or poetry published is to start by researching the market. Identify the literary magazines and journals that would be most open to your work. Once you have narrowed that down, go about finding the submission guidelines for the publication.

This information is readily available at your local bookstore or library or through a search online for the publisher or publication website.

Some tips when trying to write for magazines:

- Read back issues to evaluate and learn about the style of their particular publication.
- Look for a point of view. Are the articles written from the "I" perspective or third person?
- Consider the target audience.
- Stay true to your voice.

Trade Journals

Writing for trade journals is a fairly easy market to break into. The editors of these journals are often loyal to freelancers. This is primarily because the competition in this market is not as fierce as with consumer magazines, so an editor might not have the luxury of having an overflowing stack of queries from which to choose. As an added bonus, writing for trade journals provides a basis for you to cross over your articles to consumer magazines and newspapers. Foremost, you have built your credibility and clips by writing in a specialized market. Also, you might be able to use some of the articles you have written for the trade journals and to tailor them to consumer magazines (if you have retained the appropriate rights to your work). If this is the case, most of the writing is already done, so all you have to do is tweak what you have.

Writing for Online Sources

Writing for online sources is a great way to gain experience, create a portfolio of clips, and get your name out in front of the public. Writing on the Web offers a host of writing opportunities like blogging, discussion posts, and traditional news writing.

A great way to get started writing and build your portfolio is with websites that pay only pennies per click, but allow you ownership of the material you write. For example, when I first started writing online, I wrote regional travel articles for Examiner.com.

Some tips for writing online include:

- Keep it brief. Online readers jump around quickly and to gain their attention, you need to be quick and to the point.

- Attribute sources. As with any writing, you need to site your sources properly not only for legal reasons but also for authenticity so your readers know you have done your homework.

- Use hyperlinking. Hyperlinking is linking within your written online copy to another Web page with additional information or a related story.

- Use formatting. Break up text and make it easier to use by creating lists, bold letters, and other formatting techniques.

CASE STUDY: COLLEGE STUDENT EXPERIENCE IN ONLINE WRITING

Jordan Shoesmith
Email: jrpshoesmith@hotmail.com
On the Web: jrps.tumblr.com or joro-pash.tumblr.com

"Through writing… I have grown closer to understanding myself and my relationship with the concatenation that is our world." Jordan Shoesmith

In his own words, Jordan's writing experience can be described as "just getting started." He has been writing recreationally for about six years and professionally for about a year. In addition to writing a plethora of college papers, Jordan has also written newspaper articles, Web page content, online articles, poetry and he currently keeps two blogs. Jordan said his experience with writing "has been an existentially transcending rite of passage of sorts.

"Through writing and the necessary thought processes involved in writing — personal reflection, analytics, and the artful expression of words — I not only have developed my writing skills, I have grown closer to understanding myself and my relationship with the concatenation that is our world," he says.

In his "relatively innocent desire to impress a girl sitting across the aisle in my 8th grade math class," Jordan jumped head first into what would soon become a love affair with words in their poetic form. That love also would lead to his two blogs that he maintains, where he posts his poetic works.

"A mere crush introduced me to the then rhythmically alluring verses of your first-class, cliché-filled, cheddar-of-cheesiness poem. The sort of poem that would equate the beauty of a girl to that of an angel and would not dare fail to refer to the 'inconceivable' skipping of a heart's beat."

Now, from the puzzling short stories of Franz Kafka to the lyrical portrayal of American exceptionalism in Walt Whitman's poetry, the writing that interests Jordan has developed along with the writing that he now produces. Because of this love for the alluring poetic verse, Jordan never has stopped writing poetry and has had much experience writing college essays, research papers, and other small projects since then. Last year, he wrote for an online news source in East Haddam, Connecticut.

Of the experience of getting paid for his writing he says, "I spent the summer of 2011 writing and taking photos for the East Haddam-Haddam Patch (**www.patch.com**), an online news source under the *Huffington Post* umbrella, for which I was paid by the article. It was a very fun and informative experience that I could not have replaced with anything else."

Through all of Jordan's experience with writing and reading, he has "realized that input (reading, thinking, editing, criticism) is vital to the output (writing)." As a writer, he says, as long as one is a writer, you "never can stop experiencing what got them to where they are…. The writer is always growing closer to an understanding that simultaneously adds color to the leaf that is their personhood." With writing, "we never can stop gaining further understanding of ourselves. Writing is perpetually who we are, and who we become."

On finding time or scheduling his writing pursuits, Jordan says he just writes when he can fit it into his busy schedule. That is, unless he has a deadline to meet. "In that case, I generally think a lot about my assignment/topic weeks before beginning my writing. Sometimes I do spend time outlining my writing, however I usually just dive into my work without prior planning. That way, I take a change-it-as-you-go approach that allows me to adapt my writing to new ideas and other surprises many writers face in the process." Admittedly, Jordan sometimes gets bitten by the procrastination bug and may wait until the week, or even the day before, an assignment is due to even begin it.

Jordan does not spend time searching for paid writing jobs while he is working on his studies full-time at Baylor University. He does, however, offer the advice of "exhausting any type of friendly or work-place connections that they have already established." In addition to this, he suggests writers looking for work should browse different local sites on the Internet and perhaps even search Web-based writing sources or contract options. During the upcoming summers, he does plan to look for some paid writing assignments, using his own job-searching advice.

When asked about his favorite part of writing, Jordan said, "The final paragraph and the finishing of paragraphs is my favorite part. I really enjoy synchronizing all the thoughts leading up to an end of a work and the culminating analysis that follows. It offers the most opportunity for a writer to exhibit his/her artful abilities."

To aspiring writers, Jordan says, "find an inspiration, a reason to write, and something to write about, and then just write."

If you decide to explore the online publishing option, consider these differences between online publications and print publications:

- Word count might not be limited. Because online publications do not have space restrictions, articles can be much longer than printed counterparts.

- Keywords will become relevant. Many online publications will ask you to provide keywords with your article to accommodate search engine optimization.

- Your target audience is global. When writing for a print publication, your audience is clearly defined and you can tailor your query accordingly. However, when it comes to online publications, you are writing for a larger audience tuned into the social media trend. You will have to be more media-savvy when you query a publication and be sure to include relevant photos, videos, and sound clips.

- Keep the reader interested. The Internet audience reads much differently than the print audience. Online text is scanned more often than read, so you will need to organize your information more succinctly and in small bites.

- There is no excuse for sloppiness. Because the Internet is a dynamic environment and content can be updated quickly, it is tempting to relax on your fact-checking. It is, however, important to keep to professional standards when writing online. Readers still expect online writing to be correct and easily readable; it should be clear, concise, and error-free.

Whether writing for a print or online publication, keep your facts razor sharp. For example, Wikipedia® is considered an unreliable source for information. Linking an online piece back to Wikipedia or using Wikipedia as a cited source can easily deem your work invalid and unprofessional.

How to Conduct an Interview for any Medium

Another great way to add weight to your work is to interview an expert. Gone are the days where you have to meet face-to-face to interview a person. Now, most interviews are conducted by phone or even by email. The success of an interview is based on the script you prepare. Make the questions in your script short and easy to understand. This will elicit a clearer and more direct response from the subject. With all interviews, be sure to get the basics: names, titles, dates, contact information, professional affiliations, and bio.

As valuable as research and interviewing can be to an editor, you do not want overkill. An editor is not impressed by too many facts or too many quotes from an industry expert. Before piling all the stats into your query letter, organize a research and interviewing plan that identifies key points to convey and a few substantiating pieces of information.

Chapter 8

SUPPLEMENTAL WRITING INCOME SOURCES

"I learned that you should feel when writing, not like Lord Byron on a mountain top, but like a child stringing beads in kindergarten, — happy, absorbed and quietly putting one bead on after another."

— Brenda Ueland, journalist, editor, freelance writer

s a freelance writer, you will need to look to a variety of sources to be able to produce a viable source of income. In addition to newspaper, magazines, and online sources, a variety of other outlets for your writing work are out there. Some include press releases, ad copy, corporate materials, website copy, contract books, and even poetry and travel guides. Like everything else, always be sure to do your research first to make a successful sale.

Press Releases

Because of the economy, many companies are looking outside of their own employee pool for writers. In doing so, they are able to keep their overhead costs low, and you are able to find supplemental income. It is a win-win situation. Everyone from major corporations to local churches and government agencies need press releases written.

A press release is essentially a news brief, or simply written statement to the news media. Press releases can announce a variety of news items like scheduled events, promotions, new products,

awards, and a host of other things. Press releases also are used by businesses to help promote a new product or store opening.

A good press release includes:

- A solid headline that conveys the main thought in a concise manner
- City and date of origin
- A good lead sentence that grabs your attention
- A body that includes the basics of who, what, where, when and why
- A relevant quote or two
- The company's basic information
- Contact information for further information gathering

Samples of good press releases can be found online by visiting a search engine and typing the subject area of the press release (i.e. horse racing press release or sample press releases).

Corporate Materials

Many companies need freelance writers to write internal and external corporate materials. From website copy to press releases to company newsletters to white papers, there is an outlet for everything.

Some tips for breaking into corporate writing:

- Have a background in the corporate world? Even better, use it to your advantage to look up old contacts and use as résumé fodder to score the next writing gig.

- Look at the magazines that arrive in your mailbox. Many companies are pushing out sales materials veiled as information magazines with tips for readers that also feature their company's items for sale.

CASE STUDY: ASPIRING BOOK AUTHOR EXPERIENCED IN "OTHER" FORMS OF WRITING

Audrey Kosa
Email: amystikl@gmail.com

"I would suggest a person to experiment with a blog or a journal session in terms of feeling confident about your thoughts."

Audrey Kosa has been writing on and off for about five years. She has a bachelor's in business administration with a concentration in Italian and a master's in human development theory. She has written college papers, book reviews, poetry, Web page content, business materials, and newsletters/fliers. Audrey also keeps a personal journal and has a blog.

"I have always had an interest in writing," she says, "but lacked the self confidence for book writing, even though this is my aspiration."

Many of her job positions have included writing, manuals, seminar materials, Web content and publicity items like fliers, brochures, slick sheets, and postcards. Audrey wishes that writing items like these would be looked at as a successful form of writing, rather than the industry just focusing on your success as a "published author."

Audrey has written extensively on a personal blog for more than five years and has started a more content specific blog. She also has been asked to provide Web content four different clients including a local home schooling group, an auto body repair shop, a Realtor®, and a restaurant. She also maintains a blog for a client, with activity being sporadic as the client instructs.

Audrey does not schedule her writing time, per se. She writes when she has a purpose or specific project to be completed.

Other items Audrey has written "would include countless journals, very long, inspired pieces shared with friends in letters or email... and occasionally a request for subject-specific pieces from friends or family that have had a hard time expressing their thoughts" and would ask her to put together. For example, she has written memorial speeches for such requests.

After many months searching online for writing jobs and sending out samples, Audrey got discouraged with the process. "Online seemed so chaotic," she says, "and without magazine sample articles.... I felt I had little to offer, so I stopped pursuing (it)."

Audrey enjoys the freedom and creativity of writing and "the way in which the words come together out of my brain."

Although still trying to figure out how to navigate the world of writing, Audrey offers this advice to aspiring writers "I would suggest a person to experiment with a blog or a journal session in terms of feeling confident about your thoughts. If you are worried that someone might critique your thoughts, then don't give out your blog address, so you can keep it more private and anonymous."

Corporate writing opportunities are endless and can vary from writing copy for a customer service department, human resource departments, IT departments, and training departments. Business networking websites are a good place to get started when looking for corporate contract writing work. Websites like **www.LinkedIn.com, www.zoominfo.com**®, and **www.jigsaw.com** can provide valuable information about a company and who to contact.

Researching prospective clients and understanding their specific business will give you the necessary background to be able to pitch yourself and your writing abilities directly to that business.

Contract Books

A contract book is a book that the publishing company has contracted with a writer to write. Usually, the writer agrees to write the book at a flat fee or an agreed upon percentage of the royalties and gives up all copyrights to the publisher. Contracts vary from publisher to publisher and must be read thoroughly and understood before signing on by the author.

Some benefits of working on a contract book:

- The topic is provided by the publisher and contracted with a writer who is experienced on the topic.

- The process and details of getting the book done (like formatting, word count, and timetable) are laid out ahead of time by the publisher.

- Usually, the writer's name is listed as the author (check specific contracts to confirm), and the writer can use the book to get their name out as an established author before foraying into their own work.

Negatives to working on a contract book:

- The publisher often retains ownership and reprint rights.

- Compared to the hours of work put into a contract book, the pay rate is on the lower end.

Non-Contract Books

If you are considering writing a book, you will be expected to send a query letter to sell your book idea. But in some cases, the publisher will skip the query and ask for a book proposal. A proposal is a much more detailed version of the query. Instead of one page, the proposal is generally 30 to 40 pages long. With this many pages, you will need to cover more territory than in the query letter. Instead of simply pitching an idea, you also will need to provide information about your competition, a preliminary market analysis, and a couple of sample chapters.

Also, look at some of the following resources for examples of book proposal sections:

- How to Write a Book Proposal (**www.hiwrite.com/pro. html**): A comprehensive writing website that addresses topics such as book proposals, literary agents, query letters, and writing styles. Focus primarily on the link to book proposal examples.

- Alder & Robin Books, Inc. (**www.adlerrobin.com/howto. html**): A plain and basic website, it provides a good description of preparing a book proposal and provides links to various sample book proposals.

- Absolute Write (**www.absolutewrite.com**): An authoritative, industry website that covers all things writing-related.

Key Elements of the Book Proposal

If mastering the art of querying was not enough, now you will need to learn how to craft a winning proposal. Consider the query as a sprint race, and the book proposal as the endurance race. The proposal will require more thought and time into developing the entire strategy for your book. Five components always go into the book proposal. Depending on the publisher, there might be more, but these five should never be excluded:

Synopsis: The synopsis serves the same purpose as the hook of the query letter. The function of the synopsis is to provide detail about the book's content, structure, tone, and design. Because you have two pages to work with, you can further develop anything unique about the book such as what solution it offers to the audience, the importance of the topic, and what can the reader expect to take away from the book.

A good approach to developing your synopsis is to start with a strong, concrete opening and fill in the details later. Even though you have more room to develop your ideas in the proposal, the editor still wants to be engaged and captivated by your story. The synopsis is your sales pitch, and the editor will be asking two things while reading these first two pages:

1. Will the audience want to read this?
2. Will the audience buy this?

You can address these questions and increase the editor's confidence in your idea several ways. The key to crafting a solid synopsis is to develop your idea clearly so the editor quickly can understand what you are pitching. In addition, you want supporting evidence that will validate that your idea is a good one and that people will want to read it.

Table of contents: Gone are the days of a simple, short-and-sweet table of contents. Studies show that readers skim the table of contents to determine whether they will continue reading the book.

If your table of contents does not provide some insight into what the reader can expect, chances are they will return your book to the shelf. The trend is to be as descriptive as possible with some table of contents providing a brief summary of the chapter.

Do not be shy about drafting a comprehensive table of contents in your book proposal. Now is the best time to provide creative and descriptive chapter titles to show the editor you have put some thought into it. Editors realize that the chapter titles might change as the book evolves, but at this point in the proposal stage, all the editor wants to see is what you have envisioned for the book.

The primary purpose of the table of contents for the book proposal is to demonstrate that you are organized, you have covered the essential aspects of the topic you are proposing, and you have a plan of attack to present the information. If you structure the table of contents strategically in the beginning, you will find that by the time you receive your book contract, the writing will come much more easily.

Chapter summaries: The table of contents set the stage for how the book will be organized, but editors want more detail. Chapter summaries are an expanded version of the proposed table of contents. This section of your proposal provides brief descriptions of each chapter and discusses what each will cover. This will serve as a blueprint for developing the content when you are ready to write.

Sample chapters: Depending on the publisher, you might have to submit both chapter summaries and one or two sample chapters. When submitting your sample chapters, do not include the Introduction or Chapter 1 because often these are viewed as too introductory or elementary and do not get into the meat of the subject matter. It is best to include a chapter from the middle of the book. Whether you are writing a fiction or nonfiction book, you will need to have some chapters completed. When including sample chapters in your proposal these are not rough drafts or outlines; these are completely written chapters you will be submitting with your manuscript.

Put your best foot forward with these chapters and ensure they are top-notch. This is where the agent, editor, or publisher will get a feel for your writing style. These highly polished sample chapters are the evidence you will be able to deliver on your proposal.

Market analysis: This section of the book proposal is where you provide the platform for marketing and promoting the book. With many publishing companies expecting most authors to conduct a large portion, if not all, of the marketing, it is an extremely important exercise to develop a comprehensive market analysis. This section of your proposal will consist of the following four components:

Competition: Identify at least four to five books that are currently selling in the same market and on the same subject matter. Provide basic statistics about the book and a little bit of information about the book's sales pattern. Do not go overboard and compliment these books too much because it might take some of the limelight and steam away from your proposal. The goal is to show the editor there is a market for the topic and readers are buying the information. Find the balance that demonstrates you have done your homework by acknowledging the competition but that you are proposing a unique solution to an identified need.

Platform: Demonstrate that you have plans for visibility. This involves identifying how you will handle or initiate book signings, workshops, seminars, websites, blogs, conferences, and other visibility outlets.

Promotional plan: List various things you intend to do to market and promote your book. In this part of the plan, you will want to list radio and TV appearances, newspaper and magazine articles, website development, workshops and conferences you will be attending, direct mail promotions, and other promotional activities to get the word out. If you are a new writer and do not have any of these items secured, you can start building your promotional tools, or you can write a detailed description of how you intend to promote yourself and your book. Book publishers will market and promote well-known authors, but for thousands of other writers, self-promotion is the only outlet. Experienced writers often have a better understanding of how to position themselves and their work in a given industry. However, for beginning writers, the work to promote yourself and your book begins by establishing a website or blog, using social networks such as Facebook and Twitter, book signings, book trailer videos, radio interviews, and other creative ways to spread the word.

Demographics: Identify your audience. The demographics section of your book proposal clearly defines your target reader and characteristics of that group. You will need to list identifiers such as gender, age, income, education level, nationality, and any other characteristics that show you understand your reader.

Qualifications: Showing credentials for the up-and-coming writer can cause some anxiety. Whether you are drafting a query or a book proposal, as a novice writer, you will focus on showing you are qualified in other ways. Consider this a crash course in creative writing.

If you do not have a lot of experience or samples of previous work to provide, consider focusing your qualifications on areas such as your education, your associations and affiliations, your personal experience with the topic, any industry contacts, or your network. Without drawing too much emphasis on your lack of qualifications, the key is to draw the editor's focus to your expertise through references to professional or personal experiences relevant to the subject of your book.

If you have credentials, be sure to include them. Place qualifications that are most relevant to the book first. If you have room, add more information to substantiate your experience and expertise.

Regardless of the type of qualifications you have, a good exercise is to write a one- or two-paragraph author's biography. Reference books in the topic you are proposing and see what other authors have written. Draft one for yourself, and refine it as you gain more credits and clips throughout your writing career.

Publishing companies are in the business of selling books. They look for good, solid proposals that offer a good read and a good sale.

Travel Writing

When it comes to writing about travel, the world is literally your resource. Travel pieces can be found in a variety of magazines, online sources, and travel guidebooks throughout the world. Getting started in writing about travel will require a trip to your local bookstore. First, head to the magazine section and read the various publications on travel. What kinds are articles do they feature? What types of publications are out there? Is the writing in first person or third? Are they essay-style or more factual?

Next, head to the travel section and do the same for the guidebooks. Make notes on publishers and contact information. Then, head home and do some more research. This time, online. Is anyone out there looking for specific travel pieces on very specific topics? Are there outlets for your recent trip to the Cape? Are there specific websites that cater to traveling with the kids? Or what to pack when traveling abroad?

Create a list of possible article ideas and what may sell. Hunt down and categorize potential places to sell an article to. Research query information on an article, column, or even book idea.

What about Poetry?

Getting poetry published can be a challenge. Poetry is subjective to personal styles and tastes. What one person thinks of as poetry, another may not. Formatting, language, and creativity are the basis of many different poetic styles. In order to get poetry published, you will need to understand what the publisher is looking for in terms of content and style. If you write haiku, but the publisher prefers a different style, your time and energy will be wasted trying to get that particular publisher to consider your work.

To get started finding a way to publish your poetry, try the following:

- Research different magazines to find those that publish poetry.
- Enter poetry contests.
- Consider self-publishing a book of your poetry.
- Go in on a collaborative book with other poets.

Chapter 9

MONEY, MONEY, MONEY

"There's no money in poetry, but then there's no poetry in money either."

— Robert Graves, poet

*F*reelance writing is a business. And, as such, you will need to take time to think about things like getting paid and invoicing. A common question that most freelancers have is what to charge for their work. While most freelance markets allow you to set your own rates, writing is a bit different. Oftentimes, you write to an industry standard or a set rate as dictated by publication.

What Does a Freelance Writer Typically Make?

The million-dollar question is a hard one to answer. Freelance writers can make anywhere from a couple hundred to thousands per week. The challenge with being a freelance writer is that the work may not always be consistent from week to week; so, your paycheck might vary greatly. On the other hand, once you are established as a writer and have built up a good client-base, you can expect to earn more income on a regular basis.

To determine how much you might be able to potentially earn as a freelance writer, consider the following:

- What are the markets you can work for? The first step is to begin by looking for markets that correlate with your interests, experiences, and work backgrounds. Are you an avid gardener, for example? If so, seek out garden publications. Do you enjoy traveling and revel at retelling your travel adventures? Look for travel publications. It is not worth your effort to go after writing jobs that you have zero experience in. You always can go after those once you are established and have more time to do research to make up for your lack of experience in a topic.

- Figure out how much they pay. What is the pay range for the markets you are targeting? If there are only one or two publications for a topic you have chosen, figure out if you can expand that topic or break it down into an area where there are more publication possibilities to write for.

TIP: If you have a particular article already written, submit it to the highest-paying publication on that topic first. Then, if it is rejected, try other lower-paying publications. Once you sell it, you will not be able to sell it to another publication so it is a good idea with starting at the one that would pay you the most.

- Determine your time constraints. If it takes you a long time to write an article, you will not be able to sell as many articles a week. This will determine if the article time will give you a good pay out. For example, if you agree to write an article for $100, but it takes you 15 hours to write it, you might have been able to take on three smaller $50 articles in the same time and gotten a bigger paycheck for your efforts.

- How much time do you really have? If you have 10 hours a week to dedicate to your writing right now and it takes you an average of 5 hours to write an article, that would mean that you feasibly could write two articles per week. Do not forget, however, that you will also need to set aside time to send queries, do research, and respond to emails and that may cut into your dedicated writing time, allowing you to only produce one article per week. And, keep in mind that writing one article does not mean selling one article.

Freelance income will not start coming in immediately. Like launching any freelance career, writing involves a setup period where you are navigating and testing the waters before diving in headfirst. If you do your legwork, you can expect to start generating a steady flow of freelance work in six months. Because so many variables are involved, there is not a definitive answer to how much you can make. In your first year of freelancing on a part-time basis, you might be able to expect to make around $5,000 to $15,000, with that number steadily increasing as you build your client base and spend more time working on your writing career.

CASE STUDY:
ATTORNEY TURNED AUTHOR

Phyllis Quatman
(writing as P.A. Moore)
Author and Attorney
P.A. Moore Inc.
Quatman and Quatman, PC
Whitefish, MT
quatmanp@gmail.com
www.courthousecowboys.com

Phyllis Quatman has been writing professionally for about 22 years and considers herself somewhere between a beginner and expert. She has a B.A. in anthropology, an M.A. in education, and a Juris Doctorate law degree.

Phyllis has produced a wide variety of written work including college papers, magazines, book reviews, Web page content, blogs, and countless legal documents. She has also published a book, *Courthouse Cowboys*, under the pen name P.A. Moore.

Phyllis began her law career as a deputy district attorney in California and tried over 90 jury trials to verdict, mostly felonies. She later moved with her husband and kids to Montana, where they opened a mom-and-pop law firm in the town of Whitefish.

Phyllis' writing career stemmed out of her work as an attorney where she told "stories through opening and closing courtroom statements."

Today, she considers writing a full-time endeavor and schedules her writing in blocks of four-hour days, four times a week. Her favorite aspect of writing is "using my creative right brain to bring life to characters and story versus my daily dry linear left brain to produce boring briefs."

To other writers, she says, "write and don't let money motivate you."

What to Charge

Determining what to charge is one of the most challenging parts of being a freelance writer. What you charge has an impact as to whether you get the job, how much money you make, and sets a precedence with the client for future project rates. Setting your rates too low, also may flag you as a beginner, and you risk losing the job. Set your rates to high and the client may look elsewhere for a more reasonably priced writer. In many cases, however, rates may already be predetermined. Magazines, for example, usually have a flat price per work rate and are not negotiable on fees.

When setting fees, there are a couple of options for determining how much your time is worth. You can either charge by the hour, by the word, or set a flat project fee. Some tips on each method include:

By the hour

It would seem that setting a "by the hour rate" would make the most sense. But, charging clients by the hour actually can be very limiting. Here is why it is not recommended to charge by the hour when you are building your freelance writing business:

- Clients get scared when they hear you are going to charge them by the hour. They have no idea how long it will take you to get the project done and fear they might end up overpaying for your service.

- You will need to estimate the project anyway. If you are paying someone to work for you by the hour, your next question always will be about how many hours the contractor expects to spend on the project.

- You need to track your time. If you are charging by the hour, you will need to keep track of all of your time. Fit in ten minutes of writing while waiting for your son at his doctor's appointment? You will need to keep track of it.

- Your income is limited. If you are charging by the hour at a rate of $35 per hour, you miss making up for all of the time you spend on other tasks like bookkeeping.

Charging by the hour, as a rule, usually does not fit into the freelance writer working model.

By the word

Some clients prefer to pay by the word. When charging by the word, both the client and the writer know exactly what to expect. But, what to charge? On average, rates vary from .02 cents per word to $2 per word.

In order to determine what rate to charge, figure out about how many words the project will be and multiply by a couple of different pricing scenarios to see if the total charge would make sense for both you and your client and the amount of time you spend working on the project.

Flat project fee

Pricing by a flat project fee involves charging the client one flat fee for the project as a whole. Flat project fee pricing is beneficial in the following ways:

- There are no surprises for you or the client. You both know what to expect for pay rate.

- You do not have to prepare time sheets for your client.

To stay organized and consistent, a best working practice is to set up a fee schedule. For example, what would you charge for a newsletter, website page, white paper, etc.

Invoicing

Some publications pay upon a signed contract, while others require that the writer submit an invoice for payment. A good business practice, however, is to submit an invoice even if one has not been requested. It provides a paper trail for both you and the client.

Invoices easily can be created by using a template in a word processing program like Microsoft® Word®. This way, you can always print and mail or fax your invoice to the client or even attach it to an email.

A Note about Emailing Invoices

If you choose to email an invoice to your client, I would recommend that you turn it into a PDF or image file. This way, it is more difficult to doctor or change the original information on the invoice.

An invoice should include basic information like the date, the client's name, your name (or business name or both), the details of the services provided, the amount owed, how the client can pay you (check, money order, PayPal®), and when the balance is due.

A sample invoice might look like this:

```
Wendy M. Vincent
2 Honey Bee Lane
Anywhere, USA 12121
555.555.5555
www.wendymvincent.com
wendyvwriter@gmail.com

Invoice: 001
Date: January 1, 2013

Submitted to: Mary Parent, Wine Magazine

For: Best Wineries in New England Article
500 words @ .10/word

Total Due: $50

Payment Due Upon Receipt

Remit Payment to: Wendy Vincent
PayPal: wendyvwriter@gmail.com
```

Tips on Getting Paid

Pay rates and payment terms should be indicated in the writer's guidelines for the publication you are pursuing. If you are at the point where you are expecting to get paid, then you have worked out the terms and payment arrangements with your agent, editor, or publisher.

If you have received your payments on time, consider yourself fortunate, and continue to seek out editors, agents, and publishers who have the reputation of paying their writers on time. However, there will be times where you may have to nudge your publisher, editor, or agent to receive payment for a completed assignment.

If you find yourself in this situation, approach your editor, agent, or publisher under the premise that you are helping them out rather than placing blame. In the case where you are working with a larger publication or publishing house, the editor might not be responsible for payment processing; it most likely will be the accounting department. There also might be times where the editor, agent, or publisher is responsible for cutting the checks but forgot or is behind.

Regardless of the situation, your best approach is a short, concise email that politely mentions the oversight. Give the editor, publisher, or agent the benefit of the doubt. This will set a professional tone that will help to secure on-time payments for future assignments. Before doing anything drastic, consider these few points:

- Reread the contract. First rule — reputable editors, agents, and publisher will establish a contract with you for your assignments. If you do not get a contract, even a simple one, then find another editor, publisher, or agent to work with.

- Understand the terms. Before contacting your publisher, editor, or agent about getting paid; double-check the terms to which you agreed.

- Diversify your outlets. Try not to rely only on one or two sources for your writing income. Diversifying your markets and publications will help minimize the variation in payment and rates.

- Lessen your risk for next time. Selecting the more reputable publications will reduce your risk of getting burned or dealing with late payments. If you are not confident enough yet to pursue some of the heavy-hitters, increase the amount of research time you invest in the less established publications.

- Submit sooner. If your editor, agent, or publisher accepts invoices, be sure to invoice sooner rather than later. The minute your assignment has been accepted, send out the invoice. Be sure to include payment terms on your invoice so the publisher, editor, or agent knows how long they have to submit payment before penalties kick in.

- Follow-up. If you payment terms are net 15 days, follow up on day 16 and arrange a definitive payment schedule if they need it. Start your follow-up efforts by email first, then through letters, and finally by phone if it reaches that point.

Getting paid on time by an editor, agent, or publisher is a matter of establishing and negotiating terms in advance. Sometimes this is not possible, but it does not hurt to ask or try to get as much down on paper as you can before agreeing to do the assignment. Establish the financial boundaries during your first meeting with your agent, editor, or publisher. This is often an uncomfortable subject to broach, but think of it as preventive medicine for your professional writing career. Clear communication up front is essential for future financial dealings.

Chapter 10

THE BUSINESS OF WRITING

"You may be able to take a break from writing, but you won't be able to take a break from being a writer..."

— Stephen Leigh, writer, artist, musician

nowing how to write, search for jobs, and schedule your day is a great start to becoming a successful freelance writer. Now comes the business of writing. Do you need a literary agent? Should you have a contract for a job? What are some of the legal issues to the writing business? Should you keep all work-related paperwork? This chapter will answer some of the basic concerns regarding the business of writing.

Do You Need a Literary Agent?

At some point in your writing career you might determine that you need a literary agent. Writers, especially up-and-coming writers, can be reluctant to take on an agent because the industry average fee for agents is 15 percent. Many writers are struggling to land assignments and pay the bills, so it can be difficult to justify hiring a literary agent.

Before you make a rash decision either way, learn more about what a literary agent is and what he or she can do for you. This is as important as the research you have been conducting to craft the perfect query letter.

By definition, a literary agent is someone who represents a writer and the writer's work to publishers to help negotiate the sale of the work. These agents are paid a fixed percentage (not usually more than 20 percent) of the clients' profits. This is an important point when considering whether to seek out an agent for representation. Up to 98 percent of an agent's profits come from what you make. So, for a reputable agent, it is worth the time and effort to land you a good deal because the agent wins if you win.

The primary role of an agent is to find a publishing house that will publish your work. Agents usually work only with book-length projects, either fiction or nonfiction. So, if you are looking for an agent to represent you for shorter pieces, such as short stories, articles, or poems, you most likely will have to represent yourself.

There are two primary reasons to work with an agent if you are looking to publish a book-length manuscript. The first is that the agent you work with is your representative to the industry. He or she has the incentive to find the best book deal possible concerning money, rights, and exposure. The second reason is that many of the larger publishing houses these days will not work with an unrepresented author. This makes working with a literary agent almost mandatory.

A literary agent functions as your advocate in the book publishing world by negotiating your contract and ensuring you get the optimal deal. As far as book rights are concerned, a literary agent can market subsidiary rights to your book and is often the best person to sell translation rights, international rights, electronic rights, audio book rights, and even movie rights.

If coming out of your research about literary agents, you decide that getting an agent to represent you is advantageous, it probably is good idea. Reputable agents are experts at saving time and making better decisions at all stages of your projects. If you still are unsure and need some help to back up your decision, read this list of advantages for hiring a literary agent:

Literary agents know books. It is the job of a good agent to know about books and the publishing industry. The experienced agent will know what kind of books sell, what kind of topics are in demand, and what kind of markets are best for your particular work.

Agents are highly regarded by editors. To increase your chances of being considered for publishing, having an agent represent you is a good move.

Publishers almost expect it these days. Trends in the publishing community are moving more toward publishers not accepting unsolicited manuscripts at all. With an agent to back you up, you often have direct entry into the editor's office.

Agents are expert negotiators. Even if you feel confident in your negotiating abilities, it might be more advantageous for you to leave the negotiations up to an agent. An agent often has ulterior motives when negotiating your work. They make more if you make more. Also, agents are familiar with the boilerplate contracts for the publishing houses with which they work. These agents can quickly assess your offer and decide what is in your best interest and how to proceed in negotiations with the publisher.

- Literary agents can become a valuable "coach." Agents are not only sales representatives for writers, but they also can become your partners to success. The advice you receive from your agent can be a valuable resource for you. The relationship you build often can lead to future endeavors that will benefit you both.

- Agents ensure timely payment from the publisher. Once your manuscript has been completed, submitted, accepted, and finalized, agents will conduct the necessary follow-up to ensure any outstanding financial balances are handled. The publisher works through the agent, so any money you receive will come directly from your agent, after he or she subtracts the negotiated percentage for services rendered.

Literary agents definitely can give clients a much-needed edge over the competition. But keep in mind that agents cannot perform miracles. Your work has to be good, relevant, and have the ability to sell. Iit is your job to research the resources identified in the next section diligently and ensure you land an agent who will be a good fit for you and your work.

Where to Find Reputable Agents

The key word here is "reputable." Literary agent scams run rampant and are at the top of the list of the most common types of scams. Unfortunately, these scammers mostly succeed where new writers are concerned. You can begin your search by referencing the following industry resources:

- Agent Query (**www.agentquery.com**) offers the largest, most current searchable database of literary agents online.

- Writers Net® (**www.writers.net**) is the Internet directory of writers, editors, publishers, and literary agents.

- Publishers Marketplace (**www.publishersmarketplace. com**) is the dedicated resource for publishing professionals to find critical information and unique databases, find each other, and to do business better electronically.

- *Publisher's Weekly*® (**www.publishersweekly.com**) is a U.S. weekly trade news magazine targeting publishers, booksellers, literary agents, and libraries.

- Association of Author's Representatives (**www.aar-online. org**): AAR is a professional organization for literary and dramatic agents. It was established in 1991 through the merger of the Society of Authors' Representatives, founded in 1928, and the Independent Literary Agents Association, founded in 1977.

- Search engines: Do not forget to browse the major search engines by typing in relevant search keywords. Search engines can return countless links to excellent online resources, directories, and industry experts' blogs.

Another good approach to finding a reputable agent is to visit your local bookstore. Seek out books similar to the one you are interested in publishing. Go straight to the acknowledgments page to see if the author has acknowledged his or her agent by name. If so, you can go straight to the source. If he or she has not acknowledged the agent by name, jot down the name of the publisher. You can contact the publisher to get the name and contact information of the agent. Start with the assistant editor and explain that you are a writer and would like to contact the agent associated with the specific book. Assistant editors are used to working with a variety of authors, even newbies. If that approach does not work, try going through a writer's organization or writing group. Other creative approaches to finding agents include: asking another writer to recommend you and attending writer's conferences to get direct access to agents.

Try to stick with the resources provided in the previous sections when doing your research to find a reputable agent. Literary agents often get a bad reputation because scammers posing as agents prey primarily on up-and-coming authors as well as seasoned authors. Experienced writers warn others to stay away from:

- Agents asking for a reading fee — This is the classic agent scam. If an agent charges you any kind of fee to review your manuscript, steer clear. This practice is not considered illegal, but agents who do this are considered unprofessional and are making money from the writer, not the publisher.

- Agents asking for a retainer — Reputable agents are able to pay for their own expenses. They can determine whether a book is marketable and do not request up-front fees or retainers from a writer.

- Agents offer to edit your manuscript for a fee — As mentioned previously, agents are not editors. They should not be asking you to pay for any kind of editing. Reputable agents only will accept market-ready materials. Do not confuse the editing fee with a reading fee mentioned previously. The reading fee is charged with the notion of simply reviewing your manuscript to see if the agent will represent you or if they think it will be marketable. The editing fee is charged with the understanding that the agent actually will edit your manuscript.

- Agents asking for a commission higher than the industry standard — Reputable agents know the going industry fee, and if they try to convince you they need more to place your book, tell them thanks, but no thanks. Sometimes a scamming agent will tell a writer that because he or she is new and does not have a solid track record in the industry, he or she will need to pay a higher fee. If this is the case, look for another agent to represent you.

- Agents not belonging to AAR — Although membership to this organization does not guarantee you will land the best agent, it does provide some peace of mind because the agents who belong to this association have to agree to a certain standard of ethics and professionalism.

- Agents who sell mostly to smaller, less reputable publishers — Do not waste your time pursuing agents who have a large percentage of sales to small, electronic, or subsidy publishers. This does not help your reputation as a serious author, nor does it provide opportunities for you to pursue avenues that normally would not be available to you without representation.

Keep these in mind as you are looking for agent representation. The goal is to find an agent who appreciates and understands your material. Do not limit yourself to only the previously listed industry resources; also seek out other writers and join high-quality, online discussion groups for writers. Establish your reputation in the writing world, and you will develop the confidence to approach writers about their agents.

As you have been learning with editors, agents also have a few preferences of their own. This is why it is important for you to do extensive research to find the right agent. Your next task is to work on developing a good relationship with your agent. An agent also sizes up their clients, so be sure to have these standards when presenting yourself to a potential agent:

- Know a bit about the business. Writers easily can forget that they are in a business; they can get so focused on writing that they lose sight of the fact that getting published involves a lot more than just their literary masterpiece. Your agent is an expert in publishing, but it would help them more if you also knew a little bit about the publishing industry, too. Knowing the guidelines for crafting a good query letter, understanding the components of a book proposal, and knowing how to approach editors and agents will go a long way in strengthening the relationship you develop with your agent.

- Understand that rewriting is inevitable. Ideally, as a writer, you have come to accept that part of writing and getting published involves rewriting. Your editor invariably will ask you to rewrite your article, and your agent also will ask you to rewrite sections of your proposal or manuscript. Manuscripts rarely go to the publisher on the first submission. Do not take the rewriting personally; your agent is trying to ensure you produce the best possible book to ensure the best possible return on both of your investments.

- Be open to your agent's advice. Remember, your agent is an expert in the publishing business. He or she will know the publisher, the market, and the genre that matches best with your project. Being open to your agent's advice is a sign of professionalism and business savvy. You do not have to agree all the time, but at least give him or her due respect because it just might be the best advice you receive that is relevant to reaching your dream of getting published.

- Have a plan past one book. Agents enjoy working with authors who have a plan for a series or a goal to be a multi-published author. One-time authors are a risk for agents, so to build a solid working relationship with your agent, plan for more than one or two books. If your goal is to be a career writer, then be a prolific one, and let your agent help develop your reputation in the industry.

Seven Ways to Get Blacklisted by an Agent

Agents are just as busy as editors, so you inevitably will come up against rejection from literary agents. To avoid this, learn and commit to memory these seven ways you can get blacklisted by an agent:

1. Sending generalized queries — Agents are specialists. They help writers place work in a specific market and with a specific publisher. If you are sending an agent generalized or unfocused queries, he or she will not take you seriously.

2. Providing irrelevant information in your queries — This is boring to an editor, so you can bet that it will be boring to an agent. Providing irrelevant information in your queries tells the agent you did not do your homework. That does not motivate an agent to do the homework on your behalf.

3. Missing deadlines — This is one of the major blunders for a writer. If you cannot meet deadlines while working with your agent, do you think your agent should expect you to complete the book on time, or at all? Publishing is a deadline-driven industry. Chronically missing deadlines is unprofessional.

4. Dishonesty — Agents have heard all the stories, and they are pretty good at uncovering dishonesty and exaggerations. Be up front and honest with your agent, and you will reap the rewards in return.

5. Complaining — You are not the only client your agent has. Agents often have to manage deadlines, contracts, manuscripts, and queries from a handful, if not more, clients. If you are constantly complaining or nagging to your agent, he or she will consider you more trouble than is worth the 15 percent he or she is hoping to receive by working with you.

6. Being a control freak — You are the writer, and your agent is the expert. If you have done your homework and selected well, you should be able to allow your agent to do what he or she knows to do. Having a tight rope around your agent will not create a good working relationship; it will have the opposite effect. Be respectful, and let your agent do his or her job.

7. Unrealistic expectations about being rich and famous — The percentage of writers who strike it rich on the first attempt is low. Agents do not appreciate when a writer has unrealistic expectations about getting published. Publishing is a business and a very competitive industry. Agents are good at what they do, but they do not work miracles, and they cannot promise you stardom and wealth.

Be realistic about your goals for publishing and working with an agent. You can benefit from a great working relationship that can lead to many future successes. Just be sure to learn and study what to do and what not to do when trying to establish a working relationship with your agent.

Contracts

Understanding contracts is key to creating successful business relationships with your clients. A contract is a document that details the terms of a sale and can include these three types:

- A fill in the blank or check the boxes form

- A preprinted legal document that has certain blanks to fill in like the author's name, title of the work being sold, and the fee (and payment schedule)

- A simple letter of agreement, such as a form letter or an email

A verbal agreement also can be considered a contract, but it is difficult to contest a verbal agreement as both parties may disagree on what was agreed upon originally.

Ideally, you should always obtain a written contract. Contracts can be sent via mail, fax, or email. Regardless of the form of transmission, all contracts require signatures. Before signing any contract, you need to understand fully what it is you are signing and the rights that you have as the writer and what the rights are that the publisher will be retaining. Most contracts will contain the following information:

- The title of the work being sold/purchased

- The rights being purchased

- The medium to which the rights apply (online, print, etc.)

- Payment (the fee) and the payment schedule

- A statement regarding the publisher's right to edit the work

- The right to use the material in another publication from the same publisher or to use it for promotional purposes

- A statement that you are confirming the work is original to you, and you are the owner with the rights to sell it

- A place for the seller and purchasing signatures

- The date of the contract

If you do not understand something in the contract, it is important that you ask for clarification before signing any contract.

If a publisher does not offer you a written contract, you can always protect yourself by creating your own letter of agreement. It could look something like this:

```
Date:

Dear Publisher:

Thank you for accepting my article, NAME OF
ARTICLE. I have agreed upon your payment of
($) for first printing rights in (name of mag-
azine). I look forward to seeing my article
in the (date) issue of the publication.

Regards,
(name)
```

Copyright Laws

A copyright refers to the right to claim ownership of a particular piece of work. It means that no one can reproduce, sell, or distribute the work without first getting permission from the copyright owner. Rights are variant depending upon contracts between the writer and the client. Copyrights must be written and signed. Here are some types of copyrights generally used in publication copyrighting:

- First rights: A term that is usually combined with another contingency like "first print rights" or "first English-language rights." The publication maintains the right to first use of your material within the specific medium.

- One-time rights: Grants the publisher a nonexclusive right to print your work. This allows the author to also sell it to other publishers at the same time.

- Reprint rights: The right to print the piece a second time, sometimes called second rights

- Electronic rights: The right to publish the piece on the Internet, via email, as a downloadable file or program, or on a CD

- All rights: All rights means that you can never use that article or story again. You do, however, retain the copyright.

- Work-for-hire: You have no rights to the material. The publisher can alter, resell, publish under another name, etc., without additional compensation to you.

- International rights: Gives the publisher rights to publish your work internationally

- First-time North American rights: Gives the publisher the right to be first to publish your material in North America

Keeping Records/Files

As a writer, you have the benefit and dismay of always being surrounded by paper. You will be able to store some records on your computer, while others you actually will need to file the old fashioned way, in a drawer. Papers that you will need to keep include, but are not limited to, the following:

- Contracts: You should have a contract (or letter of agreement) for every single piece you sell. Sometimes, it may be a simple email confirming your agreement. Other times, it might be a pages-long contract the client sent you via fax. These contracts may be your only documentation down the road that confirms what rights you sold (or did not sell) to a particular work. You will want to keep these contracts forever and will need to come up with some sort of a filing system to accommodate them. You can do this the old-fashioned way with a filing cabinet and labeled file folders. Or you may want to scan all your contracts in electronically and save them on a hard drive.

- Correspondence: Email, rejection letters, acceptance letters, etc., should all be kept. These come in handy when needing to look up the specifics of an agreement with a client, and they also come in handy when organizing your business "stuff" for the IRS.

- Manuscripts: Always keep your original manuscripts or pieces of writing work that you have submitted to a client. You never know when you may need to pull up the original for reprint rights or selling to another client.

- Invoices: You will want to keep track of what invoices have been paid and which ones you will need to follow up on to get paid. A basic filing system would include two folders: one paid, one for not paid. On the other hand, if you think like me, you may want to keep all your correspondences with a particular client together and after an invoice has been paid file it with a copy of the payment in the client's folder.

- Clips: Preserving copies of your articles in the magazine, book, etc., that they are printed in is not only exciting as a writer, but also helps create a portfolio to show a potential client.

A Note on Storing Electronically

If you choose to store items electronically, it is important to keep a backup.

Handling Expenses and Tracking Income

Any money you bring in as a writer is taxable income. As such, you need to be able to keep accurate records of your income as

well as all of your busi-ness expenses. As a free-lance writer, or a writer-for-hire, the income you generate comes under the category of "self-em-ployed." Sometimes, a client will hire you on a "contractor" basis, espe-
cially if they hire you to do several projects or for a certain length of time. If that is the case, the client will pay you "wages" as a contractor and may or may not take taxes out of your payments. If you earn less than $1,000 from your writing endeavors, you have the option of treating your income as a "hobby."

Regardless of whether your writing becomes merely a "hobby," you write for wages, you become "self-employed," or a combination of the above, you will need to keep good records and look at your writing as a business. As a business, you will need to demonstrate that you:

1. Spend time writing or engaged in activities related to writing.
2. Continually look for writing work.
3. Keep professional and accurate business records, including receipts, payments, etc.

In addition to tracking your work (keeping copies of your submissions, contracts, logs of your work, etc.), you will need to track both your income and expenses. All you need to do this is a basic filing system. You even can start with two folders, one for income and one for expenses, as well as a journal (paper or electronic) to keep a running tab of your financial transactions. Some good organizational habits to get into when operating your writing business include:

- Storing receipts: You will need to keep personal receipts separate from your business receipts. At tax time, you will not want to be sorting through a mess of papers in a rush to get your taxes filed. An easy way to do this is to use an envelope system. Take an envelope and write the month and year on the front. Place all business receipts for the month in the envelope. The following month, start a new envelope, and put the other one in a file or box. Do this month after month, and when tax time comes, you will have all your business receipts in one location.

- Purchase your writing supplies separately from personal-use items. If you are buying items for both in the same store, pay for them separately. It is much easier to determine personal and business expenses down the road if you do not need to go through line items on a receipt.

- Consider a separate checking account if you are writing on a full-time basis. This is not a must-have item, but it will make keeping track of business expenses easier if all your writing-related money is coming in and out of one account.

- Keep an accurate ledger. This either can be computerized or handwritten, but is essentially just a list that tracks money as it comes in and goes out. You will want to keep track of the date, the item description, and whether it was an income or an expense item. Free tracking sheets are available online, or you could use a notebook or a spreadsheet program. I suggest doing what you feel most comfortable with.

- Records should be kept for a minimum of three years, some even recommend up to ten years. The IRS, in an audit, usually goes back three years, but may go further if fraud is suspected.

This may seem like a lot of trouble, but forming good record-keeping habits is essential for a writing business because:

1. Good bookkeeping can keep you from getting audited, but if you do get audited, it protects you since you have been keeping accurate records all along.

2. It also will help you track how successful you are at being a writer and keeping your writing business going. For example, if you are spending more than you earn, perhaps

you need to take on more clients or begin charging more for your work to cover your expenses.

3. Keeping good records of how you spend your money as a business will help alleviate stress during tax time. If you have kept records all year of your income and expenses, come tax time you will not need to scramble for the information.

When it comes to business expenses, what is deductible as an expense? Items that are directly related to your writing business are considered deductible expenses. They might include, but are not limited to, the following:

- Office supplies: Items like paper, pens, envelopes, etc., that you use to run your business

- Internet: As a writer, you will spend a great deal of time online researching, applying for jobs, and writing. As such, your Internet connection service is considered a business expense.

- Cell phone: If you decide to purchase a cell phone to use for your business (and, not personal use), the costs associated with the phone are tax deductible. A separate phone line in the house dedicated to business use also would qualify as an expense.

- Classes: If you take a class designed to help forward your writing career, the cost of the class and related items are considered a business expense.

- Dues: If you join an organization dedicated to writing or a specific area of expertise that you write about, the cost of membership is considered a business expense.

- Books, magazines: If you purchase these items for research purposes or as a reference item for your writing business, they might be considered a business expense.

- Writer's conference: The cost of a writer's conference, including a percentage of your training and meals, is considered a business expense.

- Mileage: Mileage to and from clients from your "office" is a business expense that you need to keep track of.

Business expenses are what turns into tax deductions come tax time. Money spent to run your business, within reason, is also tax deductible. Because the tax code laws change often, when it comes to business expenses, it is important to verify what qualifies as a business expense and what does not from year to year. Although, the basic deductible expenses like the ones listed above do not seem to vary much from year to year, it is important to double check what is considered a deductible expense and what is not before filing your taxes for the year.

Taxes

April 15, tax day, is when all your taxes from the previous year are due. Right? Well, not exactly. Technically taxes are due when the income is earned. When you work as an employee for another company, taxes are deducted from your paycheck. When you work for yourself, you will need to pay your own taxes to the IRS. Not to mention, you are also responsible for any state taxes required for the state you work in.

By law, estimated taxes are due quarterly, beginning in the month of April. As a writer, it can be hard to predict what your writing income will be from month to month, never mind from quarter to quarter. When you first start out, chances are, writing will not be the sole income in your household — you may be keeping another job or a spouse may be earning a regular paycheck. If that is the case, one way to offset your tax liability later would be to increase the amount of taxes taken out of your "day" job.

SIDE NOTE:

Be sure to check the current tax laws to ensure the way you are running your writing business is compliant with the law.

If you make more than the "hobby" amount allotted by the government, you will be paying quarterly taxes and will need to know about these IRS forms:

- 1099-MISC. Every client that pays you in excess of $600 in the calendar year will be required to send you a 1099 form by February for tax purposes. This form simply states the income you made from that particular client. You will need this form when you file your taxes.

- W-9: In order for your clients to be able to pay you, they will require that you fill out a W-9 form. If a client does not ask you to do so, you should ask the client for one. This form indicates your taxpayer identification number (your Social Security number if you did not create a separate employer identification number) so that what you get paid is reported to the IRS.

- 1040-ES: This form helps you calculate your quarterly payments. Your quarterly tax payments will need to be either mailed in with a voucher form or submitted electronically.

All of these forms and additional information about how to use them, can be found on the Internet at IRS.gov. I would suggest using the IRS's website to gain a better understanding of the tax laws and how they affect you as a freelance writer.

Writers, and other self-employed professionals, are entitled to a home office deduction. A home office deduction is the cost of expenses associated with keeping a home office space. A percentage of your utilities, repairs, etc., to this space are deductible as business expenses. As an example, if your home is 1,000 square feet and the space you use as an office space is 100 square feet, the deduction you will be able to take is 10 percent. Your home office must meet the following conditions to apply:

- An office for your writing business must be a clearly defined location. A spare bedroom, the attic, a closet opening, for example, that is set up with a dedicated workspace like desk is deductible office space. You cannot deduct "5 percent of the dining room table." A nook in the bedroom fitted with a dedicated work desk, on the other hand, is a measurable deductible space.

- Your home office must be a dedicated workspace that is used exclusively for work purposes. Find somewhere else to pay your bills and store your scrapbooking items.

Getting auditing is fearful for many business owners but is not actually all that common of an occurrence. Some cities are higher risk for audits than others. Do not let the fear of a potential audit stop you from starting up your own writing business. The best defense to avoiding an audit and even going through an audit is good records. If you have kept good records that are accurate and run your business in a way that complies with the tax laws, you have nothing to worry about. Some tips include:

- Keep all your receipts and never claim unverifiable deductions.
- File your receipts in an easy-to-find manner.
- Ensure that your ledger numbers are accurate.
- Keep copies of all your work-related correspondence to prove that you have been working throughout the year.
- Avoid making huge business expenses that would flag attention of an auditor on your taxes.

If your writing business really takes off, or you have multiple work-related items to claim, you might want to invest in an accountant or tax preparation company. You also might want to use an accountant if you work an outside job, run your writing business on the side, and have a spouse working full time who also has an outside business. With all of that going on, things might get complicated.

After a couple of years, however, you will become more experienced at running a business and preparing for taxes and will be able to go it on your own. That decision, however, will be based on how comfortable you become with the ways taxes work.

Insurance and Retirement Savings

When you venture out on your own, you no longer will get the benefit of an employer-driven and supported insurance package. As a freelancer, you will want to eliminate the potential of risks and invest in insurance. You may be lucky and be supported by a spouse or partner for insurance or may receive insurance through your "day" job, but if you are not that "lucky," you will want to consider investing in three basic insurances:

- Health insurance: Regardless of your age, marital status, or family, you will want to have health insurance to cover basic and unforeseen medical expenses. Currently, several options are available.

- Life: You may want to consider life insurance, which helps replace the loss of income, should something happen to you. This is especially important if you are the sole income earner in your household. A variety of plans and options are available, so it is important to do your research.

- Disability: If you are the sole breadwinner in your household, you might want to consider disability insurance to cover your family if you sustain a serious injury and cannot work.

You also may want to consider planning for retirement. Many workers are opting to work past the age of 65, not necessarily because they have to, but because they need to. If you do not want to be in this category and want to work past retirement because you may want to, but not because you have to, you will need to start thinking about saving for retirement now.

In order to plan for retirement, you will need to consider what that means for you. Does it mean you want to live simply and cover the basics like food and shelter? Or, does it mean you want to spend your retirement traveling the world? There is a difference in what you will need to put aside. You may want to consider meeting with a financial adviser to help you determine how much money you will need for retirement and what your options are to help you save for it.

CONCLUSION

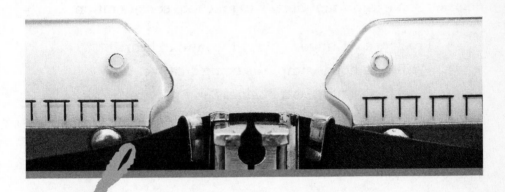

Luckily, there is no formal training to become a writer, and writers come from a variety of backgrounds. Through this book, we went on a journey through the process of getting started on your successful freelance writing career. By learning some basic skills, writing everyday, getting organized, negotiating the current trends of the business, and learning how to market yourself, you now hold the keys to turning your dream of being a freelance writer into a reality.

What we all share as writers is a passion for what we do and a basic knowledge of the business. Writing allows us the creative outlet we crave, while allowing us the opportunity to provide for our families. Part time or full time, writing can fit into our lives in ways we never imagined possible. Some of the positives of being a writer include:

- The flexibility to work around the needs of your family
- The ability to be your own boss
- The opportunity to create the life-work balance that you want

With all the positives of being a freelance writer, you also have learned some important details to take into consideration:

- Freelance writing is not for the faint of heart.
- Writing is not as simple as being creative.
- Freelance writing is a business and requires work.
- You will need the discipline to schedule your work and not be tempted by things that might distract you from writing.

At the end of the day, you need to take a look at your career and ask yourself: Is it worth it? As a freelance writer, you are sure to run into obstacles and bumps in the road along your journey. Does putting in the hours to do something you really love pay off? Do the positives outweigh any of the negatives? Has becoming a freelance writer helped you attain the work-life balance you were hoping for? If not, why not? What can you change to help balance the equation more towards the way you had hoped it would be.

I hope this book has inspired you to jump-start your writing career and go for it. I also hope that it will become a valuable resource on your dedicated writer's desk that you refer to throughout your successful writing career.

APPENDIX

Sample Business "Plans"

Generally, a business plan should include the following:

- **Executive Summary:** Includes an overview of your business idea and highlights of your business plan. It is usually one to two pages long and effectively sells your idea.

- **Company Summary:** Includes a factual description of you and your company

- **Products/Services:** A description of the products and services your company will provide

- **Market Analysis:** Summarizes customer base, competitors, market size, and potential market growth

- **Strategy and Implementation:** Describes how you intend to sell your product and how you will put your plan into action

- **Management Summary:** Offers a background on you and your management team, experiences, and accomplishments

- **Financial Plan:** Outlines potential sales, cash flow, and estimated profits

When creating a business plan for your freelance writing business, remember that you may be the only person who needs to reference it. Which means, that you do not need to be as formal as the example above. A basic business plan will help you lay out your plan for your business and keep your focus organized. A basic plan for your writing business might look like:

BUSINESS PLAN	FREELANCE WRITER
What I do	I am a freelance writer, blogger, copywriter, and editor.
Financial Goal	My part-time goal would be to make about $500 a month. If I were working on writing full-time, I would need to bring in about $3000 a month.
How I will Make Money	I will make money by writing for online newspapers, print magazines, blogging, and picking up the occasional corporate writing job to supplement my other writing.
Marketing	I plan to market myself through a website dedicated to my writing experience, call on old business associates in the corporate world, and join writing-related networks.

BUSINESS PLAN	FREELANCE WRITER
Other Details	I plan to set aside a dedicated work space in my house and spend a dedicated amount of time each week working on my writing career.

Goal-setting Worksheet

Below is a sample blank worksheet that you can copy and use to help you set short- and long-term goals for yourself as a freelance writer.

Goal	Timeframe	Completed	Notes

Online Sources for Writing Jobs

This is not a comprehensive list of available sources, but the below suggestions are a great resource in getting started:

CraigsList: **www.craigslist.org**

Demand Media™: **www.demandmedia.com**

Elance®: **www.elance.com**

Freelance Writing Gigs: **www.freelancewritinggigs.com**

Journalism Jobs: **www.journalismjobs.com**

MediaBistro®: **www.mediabistro.com**

Simply Hired®: **www.simplyhired.com**

The Write Jobs™: **www.writejobs.com**

Listing of Writer Organizations

Academy of American Poets (**www.poets.org/index.php**): The Academy of American Poets was founded in 1934 with the mission to support American poets at all stages of their careers and to foster the appreciation of contemporary poetry.

American Christian Fiction Writers (**www.acfw.com**): ACFW™ consists of authors, editors, agents, publicists and aspiring writers and was organized in 2000 under the name of American Christian Romance Writers (ACRW). In 2004, the group changed the name to American Christian Fiction Writers (ACFW) in response to the diverse needs of its membership, who write across many genres.

American Crime Writers League (**www.acwl.org**): The ACWL was formed in the late 1980s by a group of writers who wanted a private forum for exchanging ideas.

American Society of Business Publication Editors (**www.asbpe.org**): Founded in 1964, the American Society of Business Publication Editors (ASBPE) is the professional association for full-time and freelance editors and writers employed in the business, trade, and specialty press.

American Society of Journalists and Authors (**www.asja.org/about.php**): Founded in 1948, the American Society of Journalists and Authors is the nation's professional organization of independent nonfiction writers.

Asian American Journalists Association (**www.aaja.org**): Founded in 1981, the Asian American Journalists Association (AAJA) is a nonprofit professional and educational organization with more than 1,400 members today. AAJA serves Asian Americans and Pacific Islanders by encouraging young people to consider journalism as a career, developing managers in the media industry, and promoting fair and accurate news coverage.

Association of Young Journalists and Writers (**www.ayjw.org**): The Association of Young Journalists and Writers is a nonprofit organization with its mission as promoting reading, writing, journalism, and serving the community. The organization was established as the Association of Young Journalists under Section 402 of the Not-For-Profit Corporation Law as a successor to the Forum of Young Journalists, which was created in 1981.

Association of Author's Representatives (**www.aaronline.org**): The Association of Authors' Representatives is a not-for-profit membership organization, which is active in all areas of the publishing, theater, motion picture and television industries and related fields.

Authors Guild (**www.authorsguild.org**): The Authors Guild has been the nation's leading advocate for writers' interests in effective copyright protection, fair contracts, and free expression since it was founded as the Authors League of America in 1912. It provides legal assistance and a broad range of web services to its members.

Backspace (**www.bksp.org**): Backspace is an online writers' organization with more than 1,400 members in a dozen countries. A third of the members are agented, published, and include nearly a dozen *New York Times'* best-selling authors. Backspace is predicated on the idea of writers helping writers, which is accomplished through discussion forums; an online guest speaker program in which agents, acquisitions editors, and best-selling authors regularly conduct question-and-answer sessions with the group; advice; and how-to articles from publishing experts on this website, as well as real-world conferences and events.

CineStory (**cinestory.org/wordpress**): CineStory is a nonprofit educational association dedicated to providing new screenwriters with opportunities to work with committed industry professionals on a personal basis in order to raise the level of their craft and the marketability of their projects.

The Electronic Literature Organization (**www.eliterature.org**): The Electronic Literature Organization was founded in 1999 to foster and promote the reading, writing, teaching, and understanding of literature as it develops and persists in a changing digital environment.

Editorial Freelancers Association (**www.the-efa.org**): EFA is a national not-for-profit organization, headquartered in New York City, run almost entirely by volunteers. Its members, experienced in a wide range of professional skills, live and work in the United States and a variety of other countries, including Canada, England, France, India, Ireland, Israel, and Japan.

EPIC™ — Electronically Published Internet Coalition (**http:// epicorg.com**): EPIC was established in 1998 to provide a strong voice for electronic publishing. Once an authors' organization, EPIC has expanded to include hundreds of professionals from all facets of the electronic publishing industry: authors, publishers, editors, artists, and others. Members work together in a unique collaboration between authors and publishers to further the industry.

Historical Novel Society (**www.historicalnovelsociety.org**): The Historical Novel Society, founded in 1997, promotes all aspects of historical fiction. It provides support and opportunities for new writers, information for students, booksellers, and librarians, a community for authors, readers, agents, and publishers.

Horror Writers Association (**www.horror.org**): The Horror Writers Association's mission is to promote and protect the careers of professional horror writers and those seeking to become horror writers. HWA also uses its reputation and affiliations to raise the profile of the horror genre in the publishing industry and among readers in the general public.

HTML Writers Guild (**www.hwg.org**): The HWG was founded in 1994 as the Internet's leading training organization for the Web-design community, with more than 150,000 members in more than 160 countries world-wide. In 2001, the Guild joined with the International Webmaster's Association to form IWA-HWG, the professional association for the growth of the professional Web-design companies and individuals.

International Food, Wine, & Travel Writers Association (**www.ifwtwa.org**): The International Food Wine & Travel Writers Association (IFWTWA) is now a global network of journalists who cover the hospitality and lifestyle fields and the people who promote them.

International Women's Writing Guild (**www.iwwg.com**): The IWWG, founded in 1976, is a network for the personal and professional empowerment of women through writing and open to all regardless of portfolio.

Media Bistro (**www.mediabistro.com**): Mediabistro.com is dedicated to anyone who creates or works with content, that includes editors, writers, producers, graphic designers, book publishers, and others in industries including magazines, television, film, radio, newspapers, book publishing, online media, advertising, PR, and design. Its mission is to provide opportunities to meet, share resources, become informed of job opportunities and interesting projects and news, improve career skills, and showcase your work.

Military Writers Society of America (**www.militarywriters.com**): MWSA is an association of more than 800 authors, poets, and artists, drawn together by the common bond of military service. Most of our members are active duty military, retirees, or military veterans.

Mystery Writers of America (**www.mysterywriters.org**): Mystery Writers of America is a writers association for mystery writers and other professionals in the field. MWA watches developments in legislation and tax law, sponsors symposia and mystery conferences, presents the Edgar Awards, and provides information for mystery writers. Membership in MWA is open to published authors, editors, screenwriters, and other professionals in the field.

National Association of Independent Writers and Editors (**www. naiwe.com**): NAIWE is a professional association for writers and editors. It exists to help members succeed, and the unique focus on creating multiple streams of writing income can make it happen.

National Writers Association (**www.nationalwriters.com**): The NWA provides education and an ethical resource for writers at all levels of experience. This organization sponsors annual contests, offers contract reviews, manuscript critiques, research findings relevant to writers, editing services, a professional freelancers directory and more to members.

The National Writers Union (**www.nwu.org**): The National Writers Union UAW Local 1981 is the only labor union that represents freelance writers in all genres, formats, and media.

Native American Journalists Association (**www.naja.com**): The Native American Journalists Association serves and empowers Native journalists through programs and actions designed to enrich journalism and promote Native cultures.

Novelists, Inc. (**www.ninc.com**): Ninc was founded in 1989 as an organization for published authors of popular fiction. The only requirement for membership is that an author must have published at least two novels with a qualifying market.

Poetry Society Of America (**www.poetrysociety.org**): The Poetry Society of America, the oldest poetry organization in the country, was founded in New York City in 1910 by a prominent group of individuals who were distinguished in other fields.

Romance Writers Of America® (**www.rwanational.org**): RWA was chartered in 1981 to serve as a nonprofit trade association for romance writers. The mission of Romance Writers of America is to advance the professional interests of career-focused romance writers through networking and advocacy.

Science Fiction and Fantasy Writers of America (**www.sfwa.org**): SFWA is a professional organization for authors of science fiction, fantasy, and related genres. SFWA informs, supports, promotes, defends, and advocates for its members.

Sisters in Crime (**www.sistersincrime.org**) has 3,600 members in 48 chapters worldwide and offers networking, advice, and support to mystery authors. We are authors, readers, publishers, agents, booksellers, and librarians bound by our affection for the mystery genre and our support of women who write mysteries. Sisters in Crime was founded by Sara Paretsky and a group of women at the 1986 Bouchercon in Baltimore.

Small Publishers, Artists, and Writers Network (**www.spawn. org**): SPAWN provides opportunities for everyone involved in publishing. SPAWN encourages the exchange of ideas, information, and other mutual benefits. This site provides information on writing and publishing and links to research sources, publishers, printers, and the media.

The Society of Children's Book Writers and Illustrators (**www. scbwi.org**): Founded in 1971 by a group of Los Angeles-based children's writers, the Society of Children's Book Writers and Illustrators is one of the largest existing organizations for writers and illustrators.

Western Writers Of America, Inc., (**www.westernwriters.org**) was founded in 1953 to promote the literature of the American West and bestow Spur Awards for distinguished writing in the western field. The founders were largely authors who wrote traditional western fiction, but the organization swiftly expanded to include historians and other nonfiction authors, young adult and romance writers, and writers interested in regional history.

Writers Guild Of America (**www.wga.org**): The WGA represents writers in the motion picture, broadcast, cable, and new technologies industries.

Writer Resources

Absolute Write

www.absolutewrite.com

Absolute Write is a one-stop, comprehensive website for writers of all levels, and offers articles and information about fiction, nonfiction, screenwriting, freelancing, and copywriting. Absolute Write also provides information about editing, publishing, agents, and market research. The site also offers links to classes, software, and a large and active online community of writers and publishing professionals.

Agent Query

www.agentquery.com

The Internet's most trusted and FREE database of literary agents. Agent Query offers writers a literary touchstone. Agent Query offers the largest trove of reputable, established literary agents seeking writers.

AP Stylebook Online

www.apstylebook.com

The *AP Stylebook* is a style manual produced by Associated Press as an industry-standard handbook for writers, editors, students, and public relations specialists. This stylebook provides fundamental guidelines for spelling, grammar, punctuation, and usage.

Author Meeting Place

www.authormeetingplace.com

Author Meeting Place is designed for authors to meet and greet other authors in their vicinity.

Chicago Manual of Style Online

www.chicagomanualofstyle.org/home.html

The history of CMS spans more than one hundred years, beginning in 1891 when the University of Chicago Press first opened its doors. At that time, the press had its own composing room with experienced typesetters who were required to set complex scientific material as well as work in such then-exotic fonts as Hebrew and Ethiopic.

Duotrope®

www.duotrope.com

Duotrope is an award-winning, writers' resource that lists more than 3,375 current fiction and poetry publications. This resource can be used to search for markets that may make a fine home for the piece you just polished. Other services offered to members include an online submissions tracker.

Elements of Style

www.bartleby.com/141

Asserting that one must first know the rules to break them, this classic reference book is a must-have for any student and conscientious writer. Intended for use in which the practice of composition is combined with the study of literature, it gives the principal requirements of plain English style and concentrates attention on the rules of usage and principles of composition most commonly violated.

Free Management Library™

managementhelp.org/commskls/cmm_writ.htm
4008 Lake Drive Avenue North, Minneapolis, MN 55422-1508
The Free Management Library, by Authenticity Consulting, LLC, is provided as a free community resource. The library offers free, easy-to-access, online articles to develop yourself, other individuals, groups, and organizations. Over the past 15 years, the library has grown to be one of the world's largest well-organized collections of articles and resources. There are approximately 650 topics in the library, spanning almost 10,000 links. Each topic has additionally recommended books and related library topics.

Grammar Girl™ — Quick and Dirty Tips For Better Writing
www. grammar.quickanddirtytips.com
Whether you want to brush up on something you learned long ago in school, improve the way you manage your household, or develop professional skills to advance your career, Quick and Dirty Tips experts are here to help. In blog posts, podcasts, and newsletters, the Quick and Dirty Tips experts break down complex subjects to make them simpler and provide examples so you easily can see how to apply this new knowledge to your daily life.

Literary Marketplace

www.literarymarketplace.com™
Information Today, Inc.
143 Old Marlton Pike, Medford, NJ 08055
Literary Market Place (LMP) has been the directory of America and Canadian book publishing for more than 50 years. LMP members are publishing professional, authors, industry watchers, or those seeking to gain entry into the world of publishing.

Poets & Writers Magazine

www.pw.org
P.O. Box 422460, Palm Coast, FL 32142; (386) 246-0106
Poets & Writers, Inc., is the primary source of information, support, and guidance for creative writers. Founded in 1970, it is the nation's largest nonprofit literary organization serving poets, fiction writers, and creative nonfiction writers.

Publisher's Marketplace

www.publishersmarketplace.com
Cader Books, Inc., 2 Park Place, #4, Bronxville, NY 10708
The biggest and best dedicated marketplace for publishing professionals to find critical information and unique databases, find each other, and to do business better electronically.

Renegade Writer

www.therenegadewriter.com
RW discusses querying style that works for you, how to overcome freelancing fear, get motivated, figure out your own systems for getting and doing work, earn more money as a freelancer, boost your freelance writing career, and reach your writing dreams.

U.S. Copyright Office

www.copyright.gov

101 Independence Ave S.E., Washington, DC 20559-6000 (202) 707-3000

The Copyright Office is an office of record, a place where claims to copyright are registered and where documents relating to copyright may be recorded when the requirements of the copyright law are met. The Copyright Office furnishes information about the provisions of the copyright law and the procedures for making a registration or recordation, explains the operations and practices of the Copyright Office, and reports on facts found in the public records of the office. The office also administers the mandatory deposit provisions of the copyright law and the various compulsory licensing provisions of the law, which include collecting royalties.

The Well-Fed Writer

www.wellfedwriter.com

Official website of Peter Bowerman, author of *The Well-Fed Writer* and various other self-published books. The Well-Fed Writer website offers e-books, teleseminars, an e-newsletter, a blog, mentoring, and industry links.

Writers.com — Writers on the Net

www.writers.com

Writers on the Net was founded in 1995 to serve the international community of writers on the Internet. The classes and services are used by aspiring writers and professionals from Alaska to Australia, and take place either on an educational website or via email lists. There is no set time the students must "meet" online.

266 How to Make a Living Writing Articles

The courses offer extensive communication and interaction between students and instructors. Because this exchange of ideas is exclusively through text, the medium the student is trying to master, the class itself is a means of learning. Writers on the Net does not require students to purchase books or any other materials for its courses.

Writer's Digest

www.writersdigest.com

F+W Media, Inc., 4700 E. Galbraith Road, Cincinnati, Ohio 45236; (513) 531-2690

Since 1920, WD has chronicled the culture of the modern writer and continues this great tradition through relevant first-person essays, interviews with bestselling authors and profiles with emerging talent. WD also features practical technique articles, and tips and exercises on fiction, nonfiction, poetry, and the business side of writing and publishing.

Writer's Digest University

www.writersonlineworkshops.com

Writer's Digest University is a Web-based writing instruction developed by *Writer's Digest*. WD University combines the best of world-class writing instruction with immediacy of the Internet to create a state-of-the-art learning environment. WD University provides a traditional workshop without the hassle of commuting, parking, or filled classrooms.

The Write Jobs™

www.writejobs.com

The Write Jobs is a specialty job board and career resource for journalism, media, publishing, and writing professionals. The

Write Jobs is part of Writers Write, Inc.'s network of resources for creative professionals.

The Writer Magazine™

www.writermag.com

The Writer magazine has been providing inspiration and step-by-step solutions for writers of all levels since 1887. Each issue offers helpful advice for improving your writing, before-and-after examples, practical solutions to common writing problems, profiles on selected literary magazines, and tips from famous authors.

Writers' Market

www.writersmarket.com

F+W Media, Inc., 4700 E. Galbraith Road, Cincinnati, Ohio 45236; (513) 531-2690

WritersMarket.com is the Internet's most comprehensive guide to getting published. Since 1921, *Writer's Market* has been the "freelance writer's bible," providing contact information for thousands of editors and agents, tips on manuscript formatting, query letter clinics, and more.

Writer's Weekly

www.writersweekly.com

Booklocker.com, Inc., P.O. Box 2399, Bangor, ME 04402-2399

Fax: (305) 768-0261

WritersWeekly.com is one of the oldest and most respected websites dedicated to freelance writing. This freelance writing e-zine has been published continuously since 1997, and is part of the Booklocker.com, Inc., family of businesses, which includes the e-publisher and online bookstore, Booklocker.com.

Writers Write®

www.writerswrite.com

Writers Write is the Internet's largest writing site, consisting of thousands of Web pages. With author interviews, articles, an extensive guidelines database, an online community and comprehensive resources for all types of writing, WritersWrite.com is home to The Writer's Blog.

GLOSSARY OF WRITING TERMS

advance. The percentage of money paid to a writer by the publisher before publication.

agent. A professional who represents writers and markets creative works to publishers.

all rights. A publication owns all rights to the work but does not own the copyright.

APA. American Psychological Association Style is a set of rules authors use when submitting papers for publications in APA journals.

assignment. A piece that a writer has been assigned to write by an editor or publisher for a predetermined amount.

blog. A personal journal published on the Web in reverse chronological order with the most recent posts showing first.

book review. A critical commentary of a book, usually a newly published book.

business license. A permit or registration that may be

required by the federal, state, or local government to run and operate a business.

byline. Acknowledgment line that appears with the author's finished piece.

caption. A brief description that accompanies a picture, graph, diagram, or table.

Chicago Manual of Style. Known as CMS, it is a style guide for writing American English. It was originally published in 1906 by the University of Chicago Press.

clips. Published samples of writing submitted with queries to prospective publications. See also "tear sheets."

copyright. Ownership by an author over his or her creation.

contract. A legal agreement with specific terms between two or more persons or companies whereas there is a promise to do something in exchange for something else. For example, a freelance writer may sign a contract with a corporation to create a company manual in exchange for monetary payment.

contract writer. A person who is hired to write a specific assignment, usually within a specific timeframe, in exchange for monetary payment.

cover copy. Text that is printed on the cover of a book to concisely convey the contents of the book's interior.

cover letter. A brief letter accompanying a proposal, a manuscript, or résumé, introducing you and your credentials.

deadline. The date an assigned piece is due for submission.

draft. A completed version of piece that might need further revision, rewriting, or polishing.

editor. A professional hired or commissioned to edit or write pieces for publication.

electronic submission. Submission that is made electronically, most frequently by email but also by computer disks.

endorsements. Positive comments about a piece of work or writer used to promote the content or the writer's work and experience.

e-query. A query transmitted electronically.

e-zine. Electronic magazine; a magazine published online on the Internet or through email.

Facebook. A social networking website launched in 2004.

fees. Money paid to a writer for services provided.

filler. Smaller pieces of content, often in the form of short stories, statistics, or humor, used to fill in the spaces or gaps of a publication. Fillers commonly range from a few sentences to no more than 200 words.

first electronic rights. The right to publish a written piece electronically for the first time.

first print rights. The right to publish a written piece in the medium it is published in.

flash fiction. A style of literary fiction in which the author uses a short form of storytelling. The length is often fewer than 2,000 words but more than 75 words.

flat fee. Lump sum amount paid to a writer after completion of an assignment.

formatting. The manner in which a manuscript is laid out and designed on the page.

genre. Type or category of writing (e.g. mystery, romance, science fiction, thriller, or juvenile).

Google. Brand name of an Internet search engine.

guidelines. Instructions for submitting work to a publication.

hook. A technique used in the lead paragraph of a piece to grab the attention of the read.

journal. A periodical that covers news or information in a specific area or industry.

kill fee. Payment made to compensate for an assignment that was completed and submitted but not used or published.

lead or **lede.** The first paragraph of a query where the "hook" resides.

lead time. The time between getting an assignment and publication of the piece.

manuscript. Author's written copy of a book, article, or screenplay.

masthead. Printed information in a newspaper or periodical that provides the title, details of ownership, advertising, and subscription rates. On the Internet, the masthead is usually a graphic, image, or text title at the top of the Web page that identifies it.

MLA. M.L.A. stands for Modern Language Association and is a writing format and style guide that was developed in 1985. It is the standard used for academic and scholarly writing in English-speaking counties.

multiple submissions. Submitting more than one piece at a time to the same publisher or literary agent ("Simultaneous submissions").

newbie. A new writer.

novel. A work of fiction more than 45,000 words.

on acceptance. Payment given to a writer after the editor accepts the finished piece. This usually applies to nonfiction magazine articles.

on assignment. Writing a piece upon request of the editor, agent, or publisher.

on publication. Payment given to a writer after the piece is published.

on speculation/on spec. When an editor is not obligated to publish a piece that a writer was not assigned officially to develop.

outline. A bulleted list of sentences describing the major ideas to be covered in a piece.

payment. Remuneration a writer receives from an editor, agent, or publisher for accepted work.

permission. A fee paid by an individual or publication wanting to reprint a writer's work.

pitch. A detailed description of an idea for a magazine, newspaper, or book.

portfolio. A collection of a writer's works and examples of his/her publications.

print on demand (POD). Books printed as they are requested.

proposal. Detailed summary of a book, which is usually nonfiction.

query letter. A one-page letter use to pitch an idea for an article or book to an editor.

reprints. Previously published work made available for publication in other magazines of journals.

rights. Ownership of all the various ways in which a creative work may be used, applied, reproduced, or printed.

rough draft. Often the first fully organized version of a piece.

royalties. A percentage paid monthly or quarterly to an author, which is based on the cover price of the book.

SAE. Self-addressed envelope (no stamp).

SASE. Self-addressed stamped envelope with a manuscript submission to be returned by the publisher requesting notification of receipt.

SASP. Self-addressed stamped proposal, allowing the editor to mail it back to the writer.

self-publishing. A branch of the publishing industry in which an author publishes his or her own work.

serial. A type of publication produced periodically (i.e., monthly, quarterly, annually). Common serial publications include magazines, newsletters, and newspapers.

simultaneous submission. Sending a query, manuscript, or proposal to more than one publisher, editor, or agent at a time.

slant. The angle a writer presents as a way to write a specific piece.

slush pile. A common term used for unsolicited

queries sent to editors or unsolicited manuscripts sent to publishers.

social media. Forms of electronic communication through which users form networks and online communities, share ideas, personal comments, photos, videos, and information.

style. A writer's manner of expression using choice words, grammatical structures, literary devices, and other language elements.

subsidiary rights. Rights to publish a piece of work in a different format from the original work under contract.

submission guidelines. Instructions provided by the editor or publisher for submitting queries or manuscripts to the publication.

tear sheet. A sample of a writer's published work. (See clips).

terms. The deal made between the writer and the editor or publisher for publication of a specific work. The terms may include items such as rights purchased, payment schedule, and expected date of publication.

Twitter. An instant messaging system that allows a person, company, or organization to send a text message up to 140 characters to a list of subscribed followers.

unagented. A term used in the writing and publishing industry to describe a writer who is not being represented by a literary agent.

unsolicited. An article, manuscript, or proposal that was not requested by the editor, agent, or publication.

UVs. A unique visitor to a website. A unique visitor is a statistic describing a unit of traffic to a website.

vanity publication. A form of publishing in which the author pays the publisher to produce his or her manuscript.

website/Web page. A related collection of Internet files that includes a beginning file called a home page and a collection of other files (or pages) with information about an individual, a product, a company, etc.

Web search. A search for information on the Internet.

word count. The estimated number of words in a piece.

work for hire. The writer is commissioned to write a piece but does not receive a byline and does not get rights to the work.

writer's guidelines. A set of instructions that a publication expects a writer to follow.

BIBLIOGRAPHY

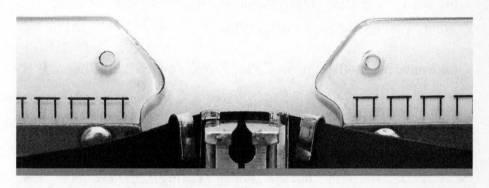

Allen, Moira. *Starting Your Career as a Freelance Writer*. Allworth Press, 2011.

Bly, Robert W. *The Copywriter's Handbook*. St. Martins Press, 2005.

Bouchier, David. Writer at Work, *Reflections on the Art and Business of Writing*. ASJA Press, 2005.

Bowerman, Peter. *The Well-Fed Writer*. Fanove Publishing, 2010.

Carter, Bonnie, and Craig Skates. *The Rinehart Handbook for Writers*. Harcourt Brace, 1993.

Fishman, Stephen. *The Copyright Handbook*. NOLO, 2011.

Formichelli, Linda, and Diana Burrell. *The Renegade Writer*. Marion Street Press, 2005.

Gibaldi, Joseph. MLA *Handbook for Writers of Research Papers, 5th Edition.* MLA, 1999.

Glatzer, Jenna. *Make a Real Living as a Freelance Writer.* Nomad Press, 2004.

Goldstein, Norm, ed. *The Associated Press Stylebook and Libel Manuel.* The Associated Press, 1994.

Goodman, Michelle. *My So-Called Freelance Life.* Seal Press, 2008.

Ruberg, Michelle, ed. *Writer's Digest Handbook of Magazine Article Writing.* Writer's Digest Books, 2005.

Schecter, I.J. *102 Ways to Earn Money Writing 1,500 Words or Less.* Writer's Digest Books, 2009.

Slaunwhite, Steve, Pete Savage, and Ed Gandia. *The Wealthy Freelancer.* Penquin Group, 2010.

Stim. Richard. *Getting Permission, How to License & Clear Copyrighted Materials Online & Off.* NOLO, 2010.

AUTHOR BIOGRAPHY

Wendy M. Vincent is a writer and editor who has worked in corporate communications and writes for magazines, online sources, newspapers, and everything in-between. She is currently a full-time editor for an online community news source.

Her past book projects include *The Complete Guide to Growing Healing and Medicinal Herbs* (Atlantic Publishing, 2011), *Working with Worms: The Complete Guide to Using the Gardener's Best Friend for Organic Gardening and Composting* (Atlantic Publishing, 2012), and a travel guide to Mystic, Connecticut (Channel Lake, 2012).

She currently is working on a children's book, a local history book, and a series of historical fiction novels.

INDEX

A